Home Sweet Home

Building Harmonious Foundations

Belal Assaad

Home Sweet Home: Building Harmonious Foundations
First published in England by
Kube Publishing Ltd, Markfield Conference Centre,
Ratby Lane, Markfield, Leicestershire LE67 9SY, United Kingdom.

Distributed by
Kube Publishing Ltd.
Tel: +44(0)1530 249230 Email: info@kubepublishing.com
www.kubepublishing.com

© Belal Assaad 2025. All rights reserved

The right of Belal Assaad to be identified as the author of this work has been asserted by him in accordance with the Copyrights, Designs and Patents Act, 1988. No part of this publication may be reproduced, stored in a retrieval system, or transmitted in any form or by any means, electronic, mechanical, photocopying, recording or otherwise, without prior permission of the copyright owner.

Cataloguing-in-Publication Data is available from the British Library.

ISBN 978-1-84774-247-6 Paperback
ISBN 978-1-84774-248-3 ebook

Editor: Sajidah Limbada
Cover design and typesetting: Afreen Fazil (Jaryah Studios)
Printed by: Elma Basim, Turkey

'After Allah, I dedicate this to my beloved parents who planted the seed of knowledge and aspiration in my heart, nurtured it and were my solid support throughout my life.'

Contents

Introduction 1

The Six Rights of a Muslim 4

The Family 6
   Family Ties 6
   The Disseverance of Ties 13
   The Violation of Five Human Rights 15
   Ownership and Control 17
   Dysfunctional Families 25

Raising Children 32
   The Rights of Children 32
   The Parent as a Role Model 46
   Finding and Celebrating Individual Talents 51
   The Importance of Validating
   Interests and Feelings 57
   Memories 60

Lying to Children 62
Showing Kindness and Compassion to Children 65
Raising Girls 67

Parents & Relatives 71

The Rights of Parents 71
Obligations 77
Advice and Reflection 83
The Forgotten Years 85
To Be the Change One Wants to See 88
Maintaining Courteous Relationships 92
Showing Concern for One's Relatives 96

Spouses 100

The Importance of Marriage 100
Parental and Societal Influence on Marriage 102
Discussing 'Taboo' Topics 104
What Does One's Spouse Love? 110
Rights and Duties in a Marriage 118

In-Laws 146

Boundary Setting 146

Conclusion 154

Introduction

The functionality of a society can be ascertained by looking at the way the family system operates in communities and the way family members interact with one another. A healthy family unit corresponds to a flourishing society, with individuals thriving and working together in harmony. In contrast, an unhealthy family relationship can become the breeding ground for persistent and invasive lifelong trauma.

Experts suggest that a dysfunctional family unit can impact up to the fourth generation, even before the need for intervention can be recognized and sought.[1] This

---

1   Psychology Today. (2024). Intergenerational Trauma. [online] Available at: https://www.psychologytoday.com/au/basics/intergenerational-trauma?amp [Accessed 19 Aug. 2024]
    LCSW, R.C., PhD (2023). What Is Generational Trauma? [online] Talkspace. Available at: https://www.talkspace.com/blog/generational-trauma/#:~:text=Generational%20trauma%2C%20also%20known%20as.

generational trauma may have ripple effects upon the rest of society and on an individuals' educational attainment, relationships and stability in later life. Especially in the case of mental, physical and emotional health, one has the responsibility to ensure that they are in a healthy state, not only for themselves, but for the sake of their family, friends and all those who interact with them.

Therefore, Islam emphasizes the importance of creating a nurturing home environment. It is a requisite of every Muslim household to ensure that Islamic virtues are taught and maintained.

In *Sūrah al-Kahf*, we learn the story of the orphans who were blessed because of the righteousness of their deceased ancestor. The scholars state that it was the righteousness of the seventh great-grandfather that came to the aid of these orphans when they were in dire need. The generational blessings one is a recipient of, and which one can bestow on others, is worth reflecting and pondering on. You may be the beneficiary of a *duʿā'* made decades ago, and your *duʿā*'s may benefit others decades from now. Imagine the reward of the first Muslim from your lineage and the reward for all those who follow in the path of righteousness.

INTRODUCTION

Moreover, it is important to acknowledge the different shapes, forms and sizes of families and this book is not here to blanket over these differences. You may find the normative family type – the nuclear family, is often alluded to throughout, and certain parts of family life are generalized. However, efforts have been made to ensure that the broader message is as inclusive as possible.

The chapters in this book are divided into sections. These sections will discuss the rights and duties of individuals, as well as the importance of honouring one's role in adhering to Islamic principles. The book aims to clarify common issues on rights and duties supported by the Qur'an and *ḥadīth* literature.

The Six Rights of a Muslim [2]

Before the rights of children, parents, relatives and spouses are discussed, the list below outlines the minimum rights we owe to other Muslims, regardless of our relationship with them. Thus, there is an expectation on every Muslim to ensure they honour and uphold these rights to the best of their ability.

1. To reply to the greeting of peace (*salām*)
2. If a fellow Muslim sneezes and says, *al-ḥamdu lillāh* (praise be to Allah), one must respond to it by saying, *yarḥamukum Allāh*
3. To give sincere advice when asked for it
4. To accept an extended invitation
5. To check up on the sick
6. To attend the funerals of other fellow Muslims

---
[2] Sahih Muslim 2162b, Book 39, *ḥadīth* 6. Also, Book 26, *ḥadīth* 5379

THE SIX RIGHTS OF A MUSLIM

We are taught by the Prophet ﷺ to be the first to extend the *salam*, and if someone says: *al-salām ʿalaykum*, to us, we must respond by saying: *wa ʿalaykum al-salām*, as a minimum. Welcoming and being friendly with others creates and maintains harmony in society. The second right is that when a Muslim sneezes and says, *al-ḥamdu lillāh*, we should respond by saying *yarhamuk Allah*, which will bring Allah's mercy on both parties. Muslims are also encouraged to advise their fellow brothers and sisters with sincere advice that does not cause them harm but instead benefits them. The fourth right due to other fellow Muslims relates to invitations to a marriage ceremony, or *walīmah*. When a Muslim extends an invitation to another fellow Muslim, the latter is heavily encouraged to attend it. If one cannot attend, due to a genuine reason, they should apologize and ensure that this does not affect their relationship. The fifth right is to visit and check on a fellow Muslim when they fall ill. If a visit in person is not possible, then one can send them a card or a text message. In this way, they are discharging their duty towards them even if the card or text message is not well received. Lastly, when a fellow Muslim dies, one should attend their funeral. These are the bare minimum rights expected from any Muslim towards his or her fellow Muslim brothers and sisters.

The Family

How would you describe your relationship with your family?

Are disagreements dealt with in a healthy manner?

When is it necessary to cut ties with them?

Family Ties

Allah's name *al-Raḥmān* encompasses qualities such as mercy, compassion and kindness. In the Qurʾān, Allah ﷻ uses the same root letters to describe family ties through the term *al-Raḥim*, literally meaning 'the womb'. It is said that the family is defined by those who are directly or indirectly connected through a shared common womb: the mother's. All the scholars agree that it consists of all those who you owe rights to, those whom you are forbidden from cutting off and those whom you are forbidden from marrying. These include parents, grandparents, children, grandchildren, siblings, uncles, aunts,

THE FAMILY

nephews and nieces. Scholars differ on whether or not *al-Raḥim* includes one's cousins and other members of the extended family.[3]

Al-Raḥim does not include the relationship between husband and wife because it is not a connection established through the womb. Despite this, the sanctity of

---

3   The jurists classify 'Rahim' as those whom are considered connected to the family tie by birth. However, they differed on the ones whom connecting ties with them is deemed an obligation into two opinions:
1. The first opinion is that the term Rahim consists of those who a person is forbidden to marry, also known as a Mahram. For example, one's father, mother, children, grandchildren or grandparents.
2. The second opinion is that it includes all relatives, including cousins. Those who went with the first opinion are one of two views within the the Hanafi school of thought, one of two views within the Maliki school and one of two views within the Hanbali school. Their argument is that if family ties meant all relatives and cousins, it would mean the entire human population since they are all children of a single womb from Adam and Eve. Those who went with the second opinion are one of two views of the Hanafi school, the more popular view of the Maliki school, a view of Imam Ahmed and the view of the Shafi'i school. At the bare minimum, all the scholars agree that the families which must be connected are at least those who share both characteristics: related by birth (*Arham*) and forbidden to ever marry (*mahram*). Allah ﷻ knows best.

As for the in-laws, step-parents/children, milk mother/siblings, they are not considered '*Arham*' who are related by birth nor connected to a common womb, and therefore are not included in the lists of the family ties which must be connected.

An important note about the meaning of 'connecting ties' is it means going beyond the minimum rights they have upon you and the minimum duties you have towards them. 'Connecting' means '*Ihsan*', to do more.

the marital relationship is highly stressed in the Qur'ān and *Sunnah* of the Prophet ﷺ and it is this relationship that can decisively influence other family ties. Therefore, it can be said that the marital bond is the nucleus of the extended family.

In the Qur'ān, Allah ﷻ praises those who keep the ties of kinship in obedience to Him and in fear of His judgement. He speaks about those,

وَالَّذِينَ يَصِلُونَ مَا أَمَرَ اللَّهُ بِهِ أَن يُوصَلَ وَيَخْشَوْنَ رَبَّهُمْ وَيَخَافُونَ سُوءَ الْحِسَابِ

… who join together the ties which Allah has bidden to be joined; who fear their Lord and dread lest they are subjected to severe reckoning; (al-Ra'd 13: 21)

Through this Qur'ānic verse, Allah ﷻ highlights that it is a religious duty upon every Muslim to maintain the bonds of the womb to the best of their ability. It speaks of those who are God-conscious in every aspect of their lives and extend their worship of Him beyond the formal, ritualistic acts of worship. As a salient marker of one's identity, this is important for one's sense of belonging in the world. Those who strive to preserve family ties are the same people who have accepted Islam as a way of life. This means that they are those who strive to excel, go beyond what is due to them, forgive others,

THE FAMILY

and overlook their faults as much as possible, Especially in matters relating to maintaining family ties.

In Islam, it is a major sin to break these family ties or neglect one's duty towards their family. However, in extreme cases, especially cases involving violence, it may be incumbent to initiate separation to protect oneself and one's family. Nevertheless, the following chapters discuss how the ties of the womb should be upheld and how conflicts between family members must be dealt with and resolved. Therefore, the focus in this book is on the majority of cases, rather than the extreme circumstances where family ties are understandably broken or strained.

In *Sahih Muslim*, it is narrated that *al-Raḥim* (family ties) is connected to the Throne of Allah ﷻ.

الرَّحِمُ معلَّقةٌ بالعرشِ تقولُ : مَن وَصَلني وصلَه اللهُ ومَن قطعني قطعه الله

'A'isha reported Allah's Messenger (may peace be upon him) as saying: The tie of kinship is suspended to the Throne and says: He who unites me, Allah would unite him and he who severed me, Allah would sever him.[4]

---

4 Sahih Muslim, Book 32, Number 6198

Another *ḥadīth* speaks about the creation of *al-Raḥim*. Abu Huraira ﷺ narrated that the Prophet (ﷺ) said,

عَنْ أَبِي هُرَيْرَةَ ـ رضى الله عنه ـ عَنِ النَّبِيِّ صلى الله عليه وسلم قَالَ « إِنَّ الرَّحِمَ سُجْنَةٌ مِنَ الرَّحْمَنِ، فَقَالَ اللَّهُ مَنْ وَصَلَكِ وَصَلْتُهُ، وَمَنْ قَطَعَكِ قَطَعْتُهُ ».

"The word 'Ar-Rahm (womb) derives its name from Ar-Rahman (i.e., one of the names of Allah) and Allah said: 'I will keep good relation with the one who will keep good relation with you, (womb i.e. kith and kin) and sever the relation with him who will sever the relation with you, (womb, i.e., kith and kin)." [5]

The Prophet (ﷺ) recited the following verses from *Surah Muhammad*,

فَهَلْ عَسَيْتُمْ إِن تَوَلَّيْتُمْ أَن تُفْسِدُوا فِي الْأَرْضِ وَتُقَطِّعُوا أَرْحَامَكُمْ

أُولَٰئِكَ الَّذِينَ لَعَنَهُمُ اللَّهُ فَأَصَمَّهُمْ وَأَعْمَىٰ أَبْصَارَهُمْ

Now if you 'hypocrites' turn away, perhaps you would then spread corruption throughout the land and sever your 'ties of' kinship! These are the ones who Allah has condemned, deafening them and blinding their eyes. [6]

Allah ﷻ speaks to the hypocrites at the time of the Prophet ﷺ, rebuking them for turning away from the

---

[5] Sahih al-Bukhari 5988, Book 78, Ḥadīth 19. Also see Vol. 8, Book 73, Ḥadīth 17.
[6] Surah Muḥammad 47: 22–23

Prophet ﷺ and choosing to spread corruption in the land. He describes how He has cursed them, and turned them deaf and blind, thus highlighting the severity of cutting off the ties of kinship. Cutting family ties affects the whole family structure, from the grandchildren, children and siblings to the mothers and fathers. Its traumatic psychological impact may be unleashed immediately, and its negative effects may be felt straight away, or they remain repressed for a while - only to manifest themselves later in life, destroying future relationships; or it may even be unleashed sporadically throughout one's life, never letting one enjoy mental stability or emotional security. The individuals who have not confronted and dealt with their own traumas may cause trauma to others.

So, how can family ties be so pivotal to a person's life trajectory?

The answer is rooted in our human identity. Allah ﷻ has made human beings in such a way that our strongest marker of identity is through our family. It is who we are, and it is the lens through which we look into the world. Through our mother, father and siblings, we have come to understand the world. The stronger the relationship is with them, the more harm arises from dissevering ties with them. Therefore, the disseverance of these ties can have painful and traumatic consequences. Disunity among family members is rarely the result of a loss or lack of love. Rather, it is due to the interference of the ego, pride, ulterior motives and the violation of rights.

Consequently, the destruction of family ties tears away our sense of self and, hence, our identity too. Beck, an American psychiatrist who studied in the field of cognitive psychology, posited his theory that negative experiences in childhood may influence the development of enduring dysfunctional beliefs and cognitive schemas, which ultimately place individuals at risk for depression. One may also feel as though this leads to an erasure of one's self.[7] Who were you before the disunity of these family ties? Who are you now? This sense of loss is impossible to ignore.

However, sometimes disseverance of ties is a by-product of life, e.g., death. Involuntary separation can leave its mark in the same way, leaving one with questions surrounding their identity and place in the world. Yet, for a Muslim, belief in Allah's ﷻ wisdom gives the bereaved reassurance that this separation was unavoidable, that it was ordained by Allah ﷻ, and that it did not lead to His displeasure. Such acceptance of and submission to Allah's wisdom is completely different from taking a conscious decision against the commandments of Allah ﷻ.

---

[7] Reilly, L.C., Ciesla, J.A., Felton, J.W., Weitlauf, A.S. and Anderson, N.L. (2012). Cognitive vulnerability to depression: A comparison of the weakest link, keystone and additive models. Cognition & emotion, [online] 26(3), pp.521–533. doi:https://doi.org/10.1080/02699931.2011.595776.

The Disseverance of Ties

Persistent and continuous effort is needed to maintain healthy family ties. A collective conscious decision should be made to address any issues and work through them together so that the family is protected from repressed resentment and bitterness.

For a husband and wife, it may become ritualistic to argue, fight, make up, and normalize this behaviour. This type of dysfunctional relationship can be overlooked and left unaddressed, perhaps because both husband and wife feel they are on a level playing field; they give as much as they get; and they resolve their conflicts in a way they have conditioned themselves to believe is adequate.

Unfortunately children, who witness this may suffer from a cognitively distorted understanding of love, relationships, conflict and resolution. The extreme importance of their initial socialisation at home cannot be overlooked or underestimated. Young children are wholly dependent on their parents for defence and protection, yet it is their eyes that witness the prodding fingers, and their ears that hear the insults, the slamming doors, and the emotional immaturity in the voices, actions and decisions of their parents. When domestic conflict between spouses is not physical, or when children are indirect victims, one may be inclined to ignore how the visual images, and the auditory evidence in their minds can creep into their life, distorting their perception of the world around them. Children are witnesses of everything that goes on around them and the imprints of the abuse they witness remain etched in their minds.

Sometimes, conflicts between the couple stem from differences in opinions regarding parenting styles or custody agreements. Children hear their names brought up and are made to feel as though they have been thrust right in the middle of the conflict between their parents. Subconsciously, the parents make their disagreement turn into an attack on their children's feelings of safety. Self-blaming begins here and the insecurities, feelings of being inadequate, and the desire to please people also begin. Often, the children become tools of manipulation, a trophy or a prize to be won, or a way to return the hurt to the one who gave it first. These consequences are not confined to just conflicts between parents but also extend to conflicts in the whole family. Children may witness their parents dissevering ties with their own parents and siblings for no justifiable reason. Children might not even be aware of their whole family tree or do not have contact with their close relatives for years.

Islam prohibits cutting off family ties and encourages the believers to actively strive to maintain them. This includes the extended family as it can reinforce their sense of belonging and identity, as well as a support network that they can turn to.

The Violation of Five Human Rights

The *Sharī'ah* has come to protect five human rights.[8] If any of these rights are violated, it becomes permissible to cut off family ties.

1. A person is a danger to you because of your religion (e.g., threats of persecution).

2. A person is a danger to your dignity and honour (e.g., sexual abuse).

3. A person is a danger to your property (e.g., they harm your property or threaten to destroy it).

4. A person is a danger to your physical wellbeing (e.g., physical abuse).

5. A person is a danger to you because of their state of mind (e.g., drug abuse, severe mental health issues etc.).

---

8 Adil, M. and Afridi, K. (2016). Maqasid Al-Shari'ah and preservation of basic rights under the theme 'Islam and its perspectives on global & local contemporary challenges'. Journal of Education and Social Sciences, [online] 4. Available at: https://www.jesoc.com/wp-content/uploads/2016/06/KC4_143-1.pdf.

We should not expect the world to be a utopia. Allah ﷻ never promised that it would be one. We are strongly encouraged to uphold family ties but, in some cases, interventions may be needed before ties can be reconnected.

Parents are sometimes forced to make harsh decisions against some family members in order to protect the other family members. This may involve limiting communication with them to ensure that the rest of the family is happy and healthy.

However, ties of kinship should never be completely severed. In some cases, maintaining some form of communication is possible. Perhaps one has a relationship with another family member that does not extend beyond greetings on Eid day, yet they know that a measure of civility is required as paths may inevitably cross. Perhaps we need to keep a measured disconnection with other members of the family and have some semblance of relationship to fulfil our other duties and responsibilities. We may send the occasional text, visit them on some occasions, or even just send them a gift. This does not have to be on a regular basis, but only when one feels it is best to do so. In all these cases, we should keep in mind that Allah ﷻ is aware of the intricacies of every situation.

THE FAMILY

Ownership and Control

In Islam, family members are connected by a shared womb. Through this connection, they share love, comfort and happiness. Unfortunately, maladaptive thinking may stem from this same connection. Maladaptive thinking is a false belief or an irrationally unsupported belief that is often conditioned and reinforced through the socialization process. A common maladaptive belief held in the family is the belief that some members own, or have the right to control, other members.

Allah ﷻ has set parameters for the relationships between family members with each other, and these parameters must be observed and respected. We are taught that we have rights as well as duties. These rights and duties are clearly defined, but they are not always heeded.

We may loudly voice our slavehood to Allah ﷻ and even repeat this statement everyday. We may state again and again that we understand that parents don't own their children, nor do children own their parents. Yet, when blinded by anger, our actions and words may be completely different to the point of contradiction. Regardless of our emotional state, we must never forget that Allah ﷻ has given us children as a trust. We must remember that parents and children are all His slaves who are bound to His laws and should, therefore, adhere to His commandments.

HOME SWEET HOME

Transgressing boundaries and violating the rights of others is a form of oppression. The use of religious texts to justify this oppression is unlawful. It is commonplace in many cultures across the world that parents threaten to invoke Allah's anger on their children because they chose to marry a spouse they did not approve of or decided to live separately because they upheld their wife's right to her own home. Invoking Allah's anger on one's children, as a threat, is sinful, and Allah ﷻ does not accept the *duʿāʾ*'s of oppressors.

In a *Hadīth Qudsī* narrated by Bukhārī, the Prophet (ﷺ) relates the words of Allah ﷻ who says:

$$\text{إِنِّي حَرَّمْتُ الظُّلْمَ عَلَى نَفْسِي وَجَعَلْتُهُ بَيْنَكُمْ مُحَرَّمًا فَلَا تَظَالَمُوا}$$

"I have made oppression forbidden upon Myself and I made it forbidden amongst you too, so do not oppress one another." [9]

Marriage can be implicitly related to this prophetic saying as it is where the violations tend to occur most blatantly. The right to choose a spouse lies with the individual, provided that this choice is within Islamic boundaries. Parents have a right to advise, recommend and counsel. Misguided notions of love and duty may make parents transgress the boundaries set by Allah ﷻ. Allah ﷻ knows the sincerity of the parents and He also knows the

---

9 Sahih Muslim 2577a, Book 45, *ḥadīth* 70. Also, Book 32, *ḥadīth* 6246..

"Transgressing boundaries and violating the rights of others is a form of oppression."

love they have for their children, but their sincerity and love do not excuse the violations they commit against their children and, often, they do not feel the need to seek forgiveness. Forcing children to marry someone they do not wish to marry, or emotionally blackmailing them to reject a spouse they are interested in marrying, incurs the wrath of Allah ﷻ. This is a very serious issue.

Allah ﷻ does not accept a *duʿāʾ* that goes against what He has commanded or allowed.

Some parents may eventually get their way, and force their children to yield to their wishes, but this means that they have destroyed a foundational element in their relationship. Children may succumb to their parents' wishes but are likely to develop resentment and anger over time. As a consequence, their relationship with their parents may become strained, damaged or even completely dissevered.

When children are younger, some parents misuse certain Qurʾānic verses to their advantage against their own children or threaten to invoke Allah's anger on their children to get them to be more compliant. However, when these same children's understanding of the world widens and they learn more about their rights, they develop a negative view of their parents. It is therefore in the best interest of the parents to never take advantage of their children's ignorance to their rights or blow their sense of duty out of proportion. As children grow in knowledge, they may become increasingly aware that the notion of 'parental intuition' and 'foresight' have been used against them. This realization may cause an irreparable damage to their relationship with their parents.

In an authentic *ḥadīth*, the Messenger of Allah ﷺ said,

$$بِرُّوا آبَاءَكُمْ تَبُرُّكُمْ أَبْنَاءُكُم$$

Be dutiful to your parents, and your children shall be dutiful to you.[10]

Parents are expected to nurture, love and care for their children, and when these children grow into adults, they are expected to reciprocate these qualities towards their parents. This mutual relationship between parents and children needs to be protected and constantly maintained. If it ever become strained or damaged, tremendous efforts must be expensed so that it can be restored and repaired. Children who are mistreated may grow resentment towards their parents and fail to honour them in their old age. Children may even see their grandparents being harshly treated by their parents.

---

10 Jam'ul Jawami', narrated by at-Tabarni in his book 'Alawsat'(1/299, no. 1002) An-Nawawi commented: 'its chain of narration is good, according to al-Munthiri' (3/200).

This may subconsciously condition them to believe that enduring their parents' ill treatment is a licence for them to get revenge when their parents are older and weaker. They may see their parents abusing, swearing at and humiliating their grandparents and believe that this is a normal relationship between parents and children as they both get older. Parents are a child's first wider window into the world. Moreover, parents form many preconceived notions about the world before their children enter it. Hence, it is their actions and words which first enable their children to interact with the world and gain meaning from it. The love parents have for their children can blind them from the fact that their children belong to Allah ﷻ, and not to them. Naturally as one builds their own home with their spouse, they may see their parents less and it is often at this point that vulnerabilities come to the surface.

In the Qur'ān, Allah ﷻ mentions those who put things right (مُصلِح) and those who cause corruption (مُفْسِد). We must be amongst those who seek to put things right and repair relationships. In some cases, some people may not deserve our forgiveness and kindness. However, we need to ensure that we are fulfilling all the rights of others.

It is imperative that, as we grow older, we build our

health, get the support we need, learn about our *dīn* and break any destructive cycles in our life. We are responsible for the next generation and so these issues need to be tackled before they are passed on to our children. We should try our best to ensure that our spouse fears Allah ﷻ so that a healthy environment and a better future are created for our children.

We will be taken to account for the trusts placed with us, whether this is our parents, spouse, siblings, children, aunts, uncles or even grandparents. Disputes between siblings regarding inheritance often arise after the parents pass away. Thus, enmity may arise over property and wealth which can lead to disastrous and fatal consequences. Sometimes, it is a sibling's new wife or husband who causes disunity, often over worldly matters. Regardless, Allah ﷻ knows exactly the circumstances we face and will deal with them in a just and fair manner. As a result, we must not embellish stories for the entertainment of others, or even create a sense of self-pity. Rather, we must always remain truthful.

We must abide by the laws of Allah ﷻ and excel in maintaining family relationships.

In *Sūrah 'Abasa*, Allah ﷻ says,

يَوْمَ يَفِرُّ الْمَرْءُ مِنْ أَخِيهِ ٣٤ وَأُمِّهِ وَأَبِيهِ ٣٥ وَصَٰحِبَتِهِ وَبَنِيهِ ٣٦ لِكُلِّ امْرِئٍ مِّنْهُمْ يَوْمَئِذٍ شَأْنٌ يُغْنِيهِ ٣٧

On the Day when each man shall flee from his brother, and his mother and his father; and his consort and his children; on that Day each will be occupied with his own business, making him oblivious of all save himself [11]

On the Day of Judgement, each individual will only be concerned with themselves. They will flee from their loved ones, those with whom they had shared all their with this life. Why would one flee from those whom they had valued the most in this world? Allah ﷻ will question everyone about their rights. These are the people who were best positioned to witness their compliance to Allah's set parameters, those to whom rights were owed, and those who can act as witnesses in favour of or against someone. There will be children on the Day of Judgement whose rights were violated and parents who used the verses of the Qur'ān for their own selfish reasons. On that day, there will be no escape from the ultimate truth.

---

[11] Surah ʿAbasa 80: 34–37

In sum, the solution to all these social and psychological ills is to become God-fearing people and treat others according to Islamic principles.

Dysfunctional Families

The Five Types of Dysfunctional Families	
The Substance Abuse Family	This involves addictions to intoxicants and drugs.
The Conflict-Driven Family	Arguments and disputes are the norm.
The Violent Family	Emotional outbursts may lead to physical violence and threats.
The Authoritarian Family	One voice dominates, and the other voices are silenced.
The Emotionally Detached Family	A superficial relationship with no warmth or sense of belonging.

(Source: Amen Clinics 2020)[12]

The first type of family discussed in the table above is a family in which addiction to harmful substances prevails. Parental figures who are addicted to harmful substances fail to cater for or be responsive to the needs of their children and this, in turn, impacts their social,

---

12   Amen Clinics (2020). Which of the 5 Types of Dysfunctional Families Do You Have? [online] Amen Clinics. Available at: https://www.amenclinics.com/blog/which-of-the-5-types-of-dysfunctional-families-do-you-have/.

emotional, mental and physical health. Similarly, children who develop addictions cause immense stress and anxiety to their parents and invite danger into the home. If the life of one's spouse is governed by an intoxicant or substance, it further makes the home a place of uncertainty and discomfort, rather than a stable and reliable environment. Therefore, the detrimental effects of even one member of the family who has lost the ability to rationally reason or process, permeates throughout the rest of the family. Studies show that alcoholism and other addictions are closely linked to domestic violence and other medical issues, highlighting the severity of the issue. (Amen Clinics, 2020)

The second type of dysfunctional family is the family driven by conflict. This is when the home tends to be a place of raised voices and slamming doors. This presents itself in the minutiae of mundane life, for example, arguments over the remote control or an item of clothing that has gone missing. The house is surfeited with screams, shouting, blame and accusations. There is no room for peace. In the long term, this can lead to severe mental health issues in these children which has the potential to affect their relationships and job prospects in later life. Psychological studies prove time and again the impact of high-conflict families on children and its link to paranoia and anxiety.[13] In particular, bipolar disorders, borderline personality disorders and histrionic disorders are found to be linked to high-conflict families.[14]

The third type of dysfunctional family is the violent family. This differs from the conflict family whose members seek conflict, mainly verbal conflict, as a means of asserting their rights and views. The violent family is characterized by intimidation, physical abuse and cathartic release. Anger is often mismanaged, and individuals may seek dominance and control in all situations. Mere imagining of the sensory overload in a violent family is enough to understand that trauma is one of its by-products. If one were to walk into the home of a violent family, they are likely to hear things being shattered and broken, or to see holes in the walls

---

13 Morelli, N.M., Hong, K., Garcia, J., Elzie, X., Alvarez, A. and Villodas, M.T. (2022). Everyday Conflict in Families at Risk for Violence Exposure: Examining Unique, Bidirectional Associations with Children's Anxious- and Withdrawn-Depressed Symptoms. Research on Child and Adolescent Psychopathology. doi:https://doi.org/10.1007/s10802-022-00966-6.

   Susan M. Bogels and Margaret L. Brechman-Toussaint, Family issues in child anxiety: Attachment, family functioning, parental rearing and beliefs, ScienceDirect, University of Amsterdam, published 2 August 2005, Clinical Psychology Review 26 (2006) 834-846https://d1wqtxts1xzle7.cloudfront.net/42509166/

14 Kaur, M. and Sanches, M. (2022). Parenting Role in the Development of Borderline Personality Disorder. Psychopathology, 56(1-2), pp.1–8. doi:https://doi.org/10.1159/000524802. https://karger.com/psp/article/56/1-2/109/835174/Parenting-Role-in-the-Development-of-Borderline

or come across black, blue and purple bruises. Children from such homes seek solace elsewhere and may run away or constantly stay outside of the home. Keeping a distance from home allows them the opportunity to seek an identity and sense of belonging elsewhere. In adulthood, these same children may shy away from disagreements by impulsively cutting off ties or they may feel the need to assert their dominance through violence, the only way they were taught to channel their emotions. Thus, the cycle repeats itself. If they happen to acknowledge that they have the mannerisms and traits of a violent figure from their past, this may fill them with a deep sense of shame and self-loathing.

The fourth type of dysfunctional family is the authoritarian family. This family is rooted in rules, commands and strict routine. There is no room here for conversation, dialogue or discussion. There is just one voice, and it must be obeyed. Such a family takes away its members' independence and ability to express themselves. There is no give-and-take in such a family as all the other voices are silenced. Rules become a safety-net and anything beyond the rules is a threat to the family institution. Such a family does not allow laughter, fun or enjoyment. Therefore, children from these families may inappropriately assert control elsewhere, such as in the school environment. School behaviour reports may indicate that children of such a dysfunctional family have issues with compliance and authority figures. Then, when the same children become adults, this issue resurfaces in the workplace, as they are unable to collaborate and work well with others.

The last type of dysfunctional family is the emotionally detached family in which there is no warmth. Members of such a family may take a road trip for hours and not share a single word between each other. They may have rules about superficial things, for example, Friday nights are game nights, i.e., a time for scheduled fun.

Despite a strict abidance to this routine, the same family is unlikely to create a comfortable environment regarding their feelings about a new job, the events of their week or their career aspirations. Children in a detached family may be subjected to egregious hours of studying, leaving them little time for play and enjoyment. On the other hand, they may be engulfed into an entertainment vacuum, likely not processing any implicit meanings or developing a wider understanding of the world around them. This may manifest in two opposing ways: either children are taught to study, before school, during school and even after school, such that the parents turn into teachers at home and there is no room for fun or entertainment; or the family is sucked into an entertainment vacuum. In such a scenario, the parents are neglectful because their attention is diverted away from the nurturing environment they should be creating for their children, and instead the children are seen as mere objects to keep engaged until they can once again be returned to the education system the next day.

These are the types of dysfunctional families that are tearing society apart and ruining the life chances of children. The unavoidable consequences of such families on society include issues with employment, education and future relationships. If the traumas suffered by members of such families are not dealt with, their future becomes bleak and cold, filled with paranoia and anxiety, as they cannot find peace in the world. These are the families which are responsible for the degeneration of society.

Describing the home of the spider, Allah ﷻ says in *Sūrah al-ʿAnkabūt*,

$$\text{وَاِنَّ اَوهَنَ البُيُوتِ لَبَيتُ العَنكَبُوتِ لَو كَانُوا يَعلَمُونَ}$$

But the frailest of all houses is the spider's house; if they only knew.[15]

As spiders are not social creatures, their division and dysfunctionality are clearly observable. The home of

---

15   Surah al-ʿAnkabūt 29: 41

a spider is made of delicate material and its vulnerabilities are patent. The types of dysfunctional families can be seen in the relationships spiders have with each other, with spider cannibalism a common feature of the species. The problematic issues of these dysfunctional families are countless.

It is the duty of every family to create a safe and loving space for all of its members. The *Sunnah* of the Messenger of Allah ﷺ, for example, teaches that eating together as a family and conversing with one another while eating is a source of blessing and a way to improve harmony between members.

Raising Children

Does your inner voice in adulthood echo the voice you heard in your childhood?

Are children being raised to be healthy and independent adults?

What factors can impact the development of children?

The Rights of Children

Allah ﷻ says in the Qur'ān,

$$\text{يُوصِيكُمُ اللَّهُ فِي أَوْلَادِكُمْ}$$

Thus does Allah command you concerning your children...[16]

Children are among the greatest responsibilities of parents in this life. They arrive in this world pure from sin, like blank pages. Parents are responsible for nurturing and caring for them and developing them, so that they become confident adults who have the best chances

---

16   Surah al-Nisā' 4: 11

in life. Muslim parents must also ensure that their children receive an Islamic education and that they themselves are good role models for their children.

Islam does not acknowledge the concept of 'Original Sin' and, so, aside from the impact of nature (genes, hormones and brain physiology), children's nurturing in the early years is wholly dependent on their parents. Therefore embracing the role of a parent means that children live a secure and dignified life and their needs are met, which include clothing, food and shelter as well as mental and spiritual nourishment. The *ḥadīth* literature offers ample commentary on this relationship between parents and children.

For example, the Prophet ﷺ said, "All of you are shepherds and each of you is responsible for his flock. A man is the shepherd of the people of his house and he is responsible. A woman is the shepherd of the house of her husband and she is responsible. Each of you is a shepherd and each is responsible for his flock."[17]

The Prophet ﷺ also said, "Your child has rights over you."[18] This is supported by Ibn 'Umar ؓ who said, "Just as your parents have rights over you, your child also has rights over you."[19]

---

17 Al-Bukhari (893) and Muslim (1829)
18 Sahih Muslim 1159
19 Al-Adab al-Mufrad 94

Before Conception

Children deserve to be raised by righteous parents who have both deeply understood the responsibility of raising the next generation.

One of the first rights of a child is that their parents have chosen appropriate partners with whom to raise children. This means that they were not blinded by love, status or beauty; rather both were able to rationally choose a spouse who they thought had the potential to be a good parent. Therefore, when choosing a spouse, they were cognizant of their duty to Allah ﷻ and determined to form a god-conscious family

Pregnancy

During pregnancy, it is incumbent on the husband to understand and be responsive to this wife's needs. He must help and assist her in every way he can, while also looking after his health for the sake of his family. He must not neglect any additional needs of his wife during this period or underestimate the changes her body goes through during pregnancy. For example, a woman's emotional welfare and hormones are linked to the baby, and her happiness or stress can affect the baby's development. This includes stress hormones and serotonin which can affect the baby too. Therefore, both parents need to learn and educate themselves on pregnancy, birth and parenthood so that they are well-informed and equipped to deal with any challenges they may face.

Newborn

1. The Right to *Taḥnīk* after Birth

Once born, a child has a right to *Taḥnīk*. *Taḥnīk* is a prophetic practice which involves placing a bit of date mixed with the father's saliva or the saliva of any other righteous person in the child's mouth. It is recommended shortly after birth. There are current medical studies which suggest administering glucose (including the process of mixing dates with saliva and rubbing it on the inside of a newborn's mouth), helps balance blood glucose levels and supports breastfeeding in the first few days after childbirth.[20]

2. Naming the Child on the Seventh Day and Offering an *'Aqīqah*

Blessing the child with a good name on the seventh day of its birth is a *Sunnah*. On the seventh day, it is also a

---

[20] Indrayani, Khodijah, H., Mudarris, N., Rahmadi, A., Anung, A., Hamat and Ali, J. (2017). How does Moslem Community Apply the Tahneek to the babies? [online] 11(1). Available at: https://pjmhsonline.com/2017/jan_march/pdf/18.pdf.

Tahneek of a newborn: a prophetic *Sunnah* and medical benefits', islamweb, dated 10/03/2008, publication number 143055. https://www.islamweb.net/amp/ar/article/143055/

Sunnah to offer *aqīqah* by sacrificing an animal and inviting people to share food as a form of celebration. Often, many couples choose to feed the poor.

3. Shaving the Head of the Newborn Baby

The Prophet ﷺ recommended shaving the head of the new born. When he saw a newborn baby, the Prophet ﷺ said [to the parent], "Take off the harm [i.e., its hair]."[21]

4. Circumcision (Boys)

The practice of circumcision for boys is highly recommended in Islam and some scholars even say it is compulsory. It has also been scientifically proven that circumcision has health benefits. Though as Muslims, we do not rely on scientific evidence to know and believe in Allah's infinite knowledge and wisdom in His rulings.

Early Years and Development

1. A Loving and Safe Environment

A child's early years start from the moment the child is born until the age of five. From birth to age five, the brains of children develop at an exponential rate, which

---

21 Abu Dawud (2839) and at-Tirmidhi (1515)

allows them to start understanding the world around them. These early years are the optimal time for brain development. The most pivotal factor for this development is the child's feelings of love and safety. Without these feelings, the development of the brain is inhibited, and this can cause almost irreparable damage in the long term. However, any damage caused at this stage can be reversed through tremendous efforts, even if its effects may have already started to appear.

The Attachment Theory focuses on the mother as the baby's primary object of attachment.[22] In the early years, the child is wholly dependent on others for their needs and the mother is often the main provider for all these needs. Studies found evidence that induced lactation is the cause of the strong connection existing between a mother and her baby. A study has also found that the production of the mother's milk is stimulated upon hearing her child crying.[23] Maternal love and affection therefore are biologically programmed. The Attachment Theory also discusses how children may look to their fathers for fun and playful quality time. However,

---

[22] McLeod, S. (2024). John Bowlby's Attachment Theory. [online] Simply Psychology. Available at: https://www.simplypsychology.org/bowlby.html.

[23] ScienceDaily. (n.d.). Newfound brain circuit explains why infant cries prompt milk release. [online] Available at: https://www.sciencedaily.com/releases/2023/09/230920111131.htm

it has also proven that fathers can quickly and effectively develop the ability to respond to their children's needs in the same way as mothers do.

Parents must be present in their children's lives and not prioritize their careers over them. There is nothing greater and more honourable than raising a human being.

For their healthy development, children must know that they are unconditionally loved. This requires parents to learn and practise patience. Children in their first few years of life deserve total patience and care. Parents must realize that their love and care for their children must supersede their feelings of anger or lack of patience. They must restrain their anger and manage it well. Children should not be made to suffer due to their parents' repressed traumas. It is not the duty of young children to be patient with their parents. Rather, parents must show ultimate mercy, compassion, love, and care towards their children. They must make their children feel secure and loved, even when they make a mistake, and not hinge their desire for perfection on their children.

Parents must teach their children to develop a positive mindset: speak kindly of others and speak kindly of themselves. Their inner voice often is the voice that spoke to them in their childhood – the parents' voice. When children are constantly berated, they may grow

"Teach them that it is natural to make mistakes and that Allah ﷻ loves and forgives."

up with a negative inner voice, so parents must teach them that it is natural to make mistakes and that Allah ﷻ loves and forgives.

2. Knowledge of *Ḥalāl* and *Ḥarām*

It is important for Muslim parents to teach their children the difference between what is *ḥalāl* and what is *ḥarām*. Children are much more likely to be receptive to these injunctions when parents have developed a loving, nurturing relationship with them. Parents must incorporate Islam in their everyday life through teaching them *Tawḥīd*, the oneness of Allah ﷻ through conversation, games and playing. Instead of lecturing their children, parents should speak with them when doing activities with them. If parents are out fishing, for example, they should use this outdoor activity as an opportunity to teach them about Islam.

3. Islamic Education

Muslims are taught that the Qur'ān is the rope of Allah ﷻ which is why their connection to the Qur'an should start at a young age. In the modern era, there are applications that can be accessed at a fingertip, something which has revolutionized the world of teaching the Qur'ān. These innovative applications with animations can help children's progress in reciting the Qur'ān fluently while also making it an enjoyable experience.

Parents should positively spur their children on through rewards and encourage and uplift them when they fall short of expectations. Each day, they should set how much Qur'ān they have to read and maintain a consistent approach. They should not threaten them with Hellfire, Judgement Day or Allah's anger. Threats of violence or using scripture and quoting Allah ﷻ to convey anger is tantamount to taking the easy route to control and curb children's undesirable behaviour.

Instead, parents should use children's early years as the time to speak to them about Allah's mercy, kindness and *Jannah*. They should speak to them about the beauty of the Prophet ﷺ and cultivate in them a love for Islam from a young age. Complex matters should be simplified for them and complex, loaded jargon should be avoided.

4. Equality

Islam teaches us that all children should be treated equally. Parents are responsible for ensuring all their children receive just and equal treatment. They must not pit siblings against each other by favouring one above another. When distributing gifts, it should be done in a fair and equal manner. Islam acknowledges that some parents may love one of their children more than the others. However, this does not warrant or excuse any unequal treatment between them as this has the potential of breeding resentment amongst the siblings and animosity towards the parents. Furthermore, when unfair and unequal treatment of children leads to psychological repercussions, the fault is entirely of the parents.

The Prophet ﷺ emphasized that equality must be applied at home, especially between the siblings. In particular, in matters such as rewards and punishments. In many cultures, parents often have a more lenient stance on *ḥalāl* and *ḥarām* when it comes to their boys. It is more culturally and socially acceptable that boys stay out until the early hours of the morning, indulge in the depravity of western nightlife and society will still harbour hope for their future. Boys, according to this stance, still have a chance to reform, change, get married and have their own families. When it comes to their girls, strict limits are placed on them. For the sake of family reputation, girls are prevented from the same level of freedom, even if none of their behaviour transgresses the boundaries of Islam. When the girls engage in the same activities that the boys engage in, they are shunned, and punitive measures are taken against them. Thus, girls are not afforded the same treatment as boys.

Some cultures may even allow a brother to speak poorly to his sister and impose his own rules on her, considering it the right thing to do. Parents will condone such behaviour, believing that the brother is raising her, teaching her and disciplining her. The son, who perhaps engages in the same activities, is, in their eyes, best placed to guide his sister regarding the issues of the present age. This is a form of oppression as far as Islam is concerned. When a man believes he has the right to restrict a woman's freedom and unecessarily place strict restrictions on her behaviours and actions, he invites the wrath of Allah ﷻ for such oppression. As a result of this treatment, the girl may grow up hating men. Whilst they have the right to advise and counsel, they do not have the right to impose their own laws in addition to the laws of Islam.

Imam Muslim relates in his compendium of *ḥadīth* the story of the father of a boy named Nuʿmān who was taught by the Prophet ﷺ to lead by example. The Prophet ﷺ asked him, "Would you like all your children to be equally good to you?

He said, "Yes, O Messenger of Allah ﷺ, I would like all my children to equally treat me well."

He said, "If that is what you want, then you should treat them equally."[24]

On another occasion, the Prophet ﷺ stressed, "Be just between your children. Be just between your children."[25]

---

24 Muslim (1623) and Bukhari (2587)
25 Sunan Abī Dāwūd 3544

As children get older and their needs become different, some differences in treatment become necessary but even then, they should still be fair and equal. The types of clothes they purchase may differ, but the responsibility still falls on the father to provide. When it comes to money, there should be indiscriminate spending on all siblings. Spending on children of differing ages depends on each individual's need and age requirements. That would suffice equal treatment. Equality nurtures love in the family and strengthens the family bond. Parents must become attuned to the changing needs of their children as they get older and be invested in their development and lives. This may mean intervening when the siblings speak poorly to or mistreat each other. Ignoring the bad behaviour of one sibling towards another is a form of oppression. All siblings deserve to feel valued and not subject to mistreatment at home. Favouritism which leads to unjust treatment is unlawful and it is the responsibility of parents to ensure that none of their children feel inferior to their siblings.

Some parents micromanage their children in every facet of their existence, thus depriving them of their independence. Unless children are too young to make their own decisions, they should have, at least by the age of puberty, some independence regarding their likes and dislikes. They should be taught to have independence over their thoughts and decisions. Parents must ensure that their children have a right to be protected, guided and counselled.

Ibn Taymiyyah is recorded to have said that forced marriages go against not only Islam, but logic too. This is because Islam emphasizes the idea of having autonomy over one's decisions and actions. Regarding this, Ibn Taymiyyah said, "Allah did not allow her parents/guardian to oblige her to buy, sell, eat a particular food or drink without her permission, or wear a certain outfit which she does not desire." Hereby, highlighting the importance of independent decision-making skills.[26]

It is important to distinguish between self-entitled, undisciplined children and children who are merely expressing their opinion on a certain matter. Parents can advise and recommend a certain course of action, but they should not control or force their children to obey them. Children must also be taught to learn for themselves and make their own choices. They must learn to respect their parents' authority over them while also recognizing their independence and taking responsibility for their actions.

---

[26] Majmu' al-Fatawa, jurisprudence, the book of Nikah (32 / 22-25) Also see, islamweb.net, Islamic Library, ch 32, page 23

The Parent as a Role Model

Children's early childhood is limited and their first interactions with the world come from their parents. As they develop, children mimic their parents' smile and laughter, and babble and coo in response to their speech.

Studies show that babies in their first year can distinguish positive and negative sounds to such an extent that hearing raised voices can distress them, leading them to cry.[27] Between the ages of two and seven, children start to establish their own identity and character. Their mannerisms start reflecting those of their parents and they look up to them for guidance. As teenagers, they may not always ask for help when navigating crossroads, but they have already subconsciously factored their parents in as part of their decision-making process. They use their parents for help and guidance, even when they do not ask them directly.

Furthermore, creating a semblance of infallibility can be as damaging as making mistakes repeatedly. Hence,

---

[27] Gattis, M., Weinstein, N. and Gerson, S. (2017). Before babies understand words, they understand tones of voice. [online] The Conversation. Available at: https://theconversation.com/before-babies-understand-words-they-understand-tones-of-voice-81978#:~:text=Studies%20have%20also%20confirmed%20that [Accessed 23 Aug. 2024].

Fernald, A. (1993). Approval and Disapproval: Infant Responsiveness to Vocal Affect in Familiar and Unfamiliar Languages. Child Development, 64(3), p.657. doi:https://doi.org/10.2307/1131209.

letting children know their parents make mistakes, but constantly strive to rectify the errors of their ways, is a necessary component of their development. Parents must show their children affection and care and let them know it is fine to make mistakes while also teaching them the importance of seeking forgiveness.

It is also important that parents are consistent in their approach and work as a team. This means they always demonstrate a united front. Allowing one parent to play the role of the 'good cop' and the other, the role of the 'bad cop', damages a child's relationship with their parents. Decisions on how discipline is administered at home must be taken by both parents.

Children also need routine, and parents need to be firm with them. A liberal approach to how children behave at home creates lazy children who grow up feeling self-entitled and expecting the world to yield to every whim of theirs. Children need to wake up in time for school, and not be excused by their parents when they arrive late or are half asleep.

It is assumed that children have an automatic respect for their parents. However, respect for their authority when parents have an inconsistent approach in raising their children, diminishes. Furthermore, violence at home and the inability to channel negative feelings appropriately can distance children from their parents. Sometimes this distancing is manifested in a physical form, but it can also be verbal, emotional, mental or even through the manipulation of religious texts. Oftentimes, parents quote scripture to their children to make them respond to their wishes; sometimes they shout, scream, call them names or throw objects around to assert their dominance. They may attempt to invoke Allah's wrath on their children just to get their way or they may subject their children to a long period of the silent treatment as a punishment. Bad role models are emotionally distant and immature, as well as unresponsive to the needs and cries of their children. Can one imagine the harm of emotionally distant parents? Such parents may lead their children to having low self-esteem, not being able to stand up for themselves and not able to hold authority in their voice, even when speaking the truth.

Muslims are taught that obedience to Allah ﷻ supersedes their obedience to His creation. Parents must ensure that their instructions and advice comply with Islamic principles. They must be wary of factors that can make them lose their children's trust and respect. Violent, manipulative, dishonest and inconsistent parents, who may even speak poorly of each other, may imprint in the minds of their children that the home is not a safe space. They may feel their voices are not heard but are, instead, given lectures and ordered around. These children will be deprived of their own independence and view themselves through their parents' words. Even when they are right, their personality would be so weak that they would find it difficult to assert their voice.

The Prophet ﷺ was not afraid of showing his humility. It is stated in the Biographies of Ibn Hisham and in *Bidaya Wannihaya* by Ibn Kathir that the Prophet ﷺ was straightening up the rows in preparation for prayer on the fields of Badr. In his hand was a blunt arrow when he saw a man disorganized in his row named Sawwad bin Ghaziah al-Ansari. The Prophet ﷺ poked him lightly with it on his belly jokingly to move into line saying, "Stand right, O Sawwad". Sawwad replied jokingly, "O Messenger of Allah ﷺ, you hurt me! Allah ﷻ has sent you in truth and to apply justice, so let me take back my right." The Prophet ﷺ lifted his shirt, revealing his blessed stomach, at which Sawwad hugged the Prophet ﷺ and then kissed his stomach instead. When the Prophet ﷺ asked why he did that, the man replied, "O Messenger of Allah ﷺ, as you can see we are here about to go into battle. I wanted my contact with you to be my last moments in life." The Prophet ﷺ then made *du'a'* for him.[28]

---

[28] Abdul Malik ibn Hisham, The Biography of the Prophet by Ibn Hisham, book 2, page 278-279 And Islamweb.net, 05/04/2015, number. 202741.

HOME SWEET HOME

Parents usually fret about their children's safety, and even when this is not a factor, they worry about their immune system. This may mean that parents prefer to keep their children indoors and occupy their time with television or electronic devices. However, children's immune system, creativity and connection to nature is strengthened through outdoor play and so effort should be made to try create a safe outdoor environment.

Anas Ibn Mālik was left with the Prophet ﷺ by his mother to serve and learn from him for ten years. He reported that he never heard the Prophet ﷺ say, "Fie, why did you do that?" or "Why did you not do that?" and that he never put him down. He reported that one day, when he was about ten, the Prophet ﷺ sent him on an errand. He said, "And then I got caught up watching children playing. I forgot about the errand, and I was just watching." Like a child, Anas Ibn Mālik reported his error of being distracted. He reported that he then heard the Prophet ﷺ behind him laughing and smiling as he said, "What happened to the errand, Anas?"

And Anas Ibn Mālik reported that he said, "I'm going now."

The Prophet ﷺ responded, "Very well, do not worry. You can play. Just do the errand."[29]

---

[29] Sahih Muslim, book 30, number 5724

RAISING CHILDREN

The gentleness of the Prophet's approach can be clearly seen here. He did not scold him or make him feel inferior; he accepted that it is in the nature of a child to be distracted. Still, he reminded him about his duty and that he has an errand to do, showing that there was still an expectation to be upheld.

This mental strength needs to be cultivated in children – they should know that they can mess up but still be loved, nurtured and cared for. In this way, they will develop resilience in their own lives and become reminders for their parents that they are not perfect, just as their parents themselves are not.

Parents must be the role models they want their children to follow. They must embody what they teach before they preach.

Finding and Celebrating Individual Talents

لَـقَدْ كَانَ لَكُمْ فِيْ رَسُوْلِ اللّٰهِ اُسْوَةٌ حَسَنَةٌ لَّمَنْ كَانَ يَرْجُو اللّٰـهَ وَالْيَوْمَ الْاٰخِرَ وَذَكَـرَ اللّٰـهَ كَثِيْـرًا

Surely there was a good example for you in the Messenger of Allah, for all those who look forward to Allah and the Last Day and remember Allah much.[30]

---

30 Surah al-Zumar 33: 21

For whom is the Prophet Muḥammad ﷺ the best example?

He is the best example for those who remember Allah ﷻ, connect to Him, believe in Him, and fear and love Him. He is an example for those who anticipate attaining Paradise and meeting Allah ﷻ in the Hereafter. Allah ﷻ highlights how we should look up to the Prophet ﷺ as a guide in all matters, including how we raise our children. As his life is well-documented, we are in a privileged position to benefit from being among his followers.

Accepting that he was a Messenger of Allah ﷻ and that he will be mankind's intercessor in the Hereafter is a critical component of one's faith. Muslims are taught to remember Allah ﷻ at all times, and to ask Him for guidance and accept the guidance He has already sent.

The following narrations focus on the Prophet's interactions with young people in his community. The first example is between the Prophet ﷺ and a teenager named Abū Maḥdhūrah. It is important to note that teenagers often have a spike in many key hormones during their developmental stage. Moreover, their prefrontal cortex, responsible for logical reasoning and rational decision-making, is still in its developmental stage. Likewise, teenagers are often labelled and characterized for their reckless and impulsive behaviours.

Even more so, they are often seen as a collective threat to society's norms and values because they tend to push the boundaries set by society. Despite being old enough to make autonomous decisions on many affairs in their lives, teenagers are also very susceptible to falling for the demands of peer pressure. In the following narration, we see how these factors come into play.

Abū Maḥdhūrah narrated an incident that happened when he was still a disbeliever. The episode took place in Makkah, after the Prophet ﷺ had conquered it and promised its inhabitants that no harm shall come to them. Despite this promise, there were still many who hated Islam, especially due to the change it meant for a society they had known their whole lives. Among those who felt this way was Abū Maḥdhūrah and his friends.

As a teenager living in Makkah – a place he felt a strong sense of belonging to as his parents were also from Makkah – he related the following: "The Prophet ﷺ left Makkah for the Battle of *Ḥunayn* and we thought he was out of Makkah.

As I was walking towards Makkah with a group of my friends, the Prophet ﷺ entered Makkah without us knowing. As it was time for prayer, the Prophet ﷺ asked one of his *mu'adhdhin*s to call the *adhān*.

When the *mu'adhdhin* called the *adhān* in Makkah, my friends and I began to tease and mock the *mu'adhdhin*. We started to mimic it and raise our voices, making all sorts of noises. My friends started to mock the *adhān* and the way *Allāhu Akbar* was said. My voice was the loudest and stood out from amongst the voices of my friends, and I had a nice voice. I had a clear, loud voice.

As we got closer, the Prophet ﷺ heard us. So, he sent his companions to take us to him. When I stood in front of the Prophet ﷺ I could not bring myself to look at his face. I thought he was going to kill us because he and his companions had just come from the battlefield and had their swords with them. He came up to us and said, "Which one of you was raising his voice the most?" All my friends pointed to me. The Prophet ﷺ dismissed all my friends so we remained alone. He did not say a single bad word to them. He simply said, "Just go and leave me with this Abū Maḥdhūrah."

He said to me, "Come here, Abū Maḥdhūrah. Were you the one with the loud voice?"

I said, "Yes."

He said, "I found your voice impressive. It is actually very nice. You have a talent, young man." And he smiled at me. This was not what I expected, and I thought about how everyone around me told me he was a bad man.

He then took a little bag and gave it to me.

I looked in the bag and it had some silver coins. And he said to me, "I want you to repeat after me these words."

He asked me to repeat after him, "*Allāhu Akbar, Allāhu Akbar.*"

I repeated after him and he said, "You have got to raise your voice the way you were doing it before." So, I raised my voice and went through the entire *adhān* until he finished it. And I memorized the *adhān* the way the Prophet ﷺ taught me with my loud and far-reaching, distinctive voice. And then he put his hand on my forehead and wiped it, and then wiped over my face gently. Then he wiped over my chest where my heart is placed. And then he wiped over where my liver is and then over my stomach.

He said to me, 'May Allah ﷻ bless through you, and may Allah ﷻ make you a blessing." And then once I left, I thought about what he had said.

I came back and asked him about Islam. After the incident, the man I hated the most in the world became the one who was most beloved to me. And the *adhān* which I had hated, became the most beloved to me.

And I said to him, "I bear witness that there is only one God worthy of worship, and you are His Messenger."

I thought about the bag of coins he had given me and asked him, "O Messenger of Allah ﷺ, are you trying to employ me? Is that why you gave me the bag?"

And he said, "Yes, do you accept the offer?"

And I said, "Yes, I do."

He said, "I've employed you as the main *mu'adhdhin* of Makkah."[31]

This is the story of how Abū Maḥdhūrah ؓ became the fourth *mu'adhdhin* of Makkah. From his teenage years until his death at the age of fifty-nine, he called the *adhān* for people to head to the mosque to pray. We also often hear the story of how Bilāl ؓ became a *mu'adhdhin* and how he called the *adhān* in Madinah.

Through these examples, we learn how the Islamic tradition holds the *mu'adhdhin*s in a very honourable position and how the Prophet ﷺ was a great leader who was able to see the potential in others. He did not judge or reprimand Abū Maḥdhūrah ؓ. He knew that this teenager's tender age made him susceptible to mistakes and misjudgements. He also knew that he was probably influenced by his peer group. He saw beyond the jokes and the laughter; he saw the heart of Abū

---

31 Sunan an-Nasa'i 632, Book 7, *hadīth*s 7 & 8. Also (English translation) Vol. 1, Book 7, *ḥadīth* 633 & 634

Maḥdhūrah ﷺ and he directed him towards something good. This is an important reminder for those who are around children daily. One should try to showcase their talents, celebrate them and make them feel valued. Celebrating individual talents is a prophetic characteristic amply demonstrated in the *Sīrah* of the Prophet ﷺ.

The Importance of Validating Interests and Feelings

Allah ﷻ says,

$$وَمَا أَرْسَلْنَاكَ إِلَّا رَحْمَةً لِلْعَالَمِينَ$$

We have sent you forth as nothing but mercy to people of the whole world.[32]

The Prophet ﷺ was known for his good character and gentle treatment of others. Children in his community knew him for his smile and cheerful face.

His blessed presence was also felt by children. Many narrations from children describe the Prophet's face, especially his smile. The Prophet ﷺ always made children feel loved and valued. As demonstrated in the following *ḥadīth*, children often notice minute details and, when they feel safe, they often express their thoughts.

---

32 Surah al-Anbiyā' 21: 107

HOME SWEET HOME

Their curiosity and inquisitiveness, prompted by their young age, meant they did not feel the same level of shyness towards the Prophet ﷺ that many adult narrators had felt. Adult companions often reported that they were unable to narrate details of the Prophet's appearance because in his presence, they were overwhelmed and in awe of him.

Anas ؓ, who was very young, when he served the Prophet ﷺ, narrated the following incident between his younger brother Abū 'Umayr ؓ and the Prophet ﷺ. He said,

"I had a brother who was younger than me, a toddler who had not been weaned long ago. He had a bird called 'Nughayr', which was like a sparrow. Whenever the Prophet ﷺ saw my brother, he would smile and ask him, "O Abū 'Umayr, what did the Nughayr do?"

One day, the bird died and the Prophet ﷺ saw Abū 'Umayr crying. So he went up to him, sat with him, put his arms around him, and said, "Tell me about the bird."[33]

Through this incident, we can see how the Prophet ﷺ validated the young boy's feelings and connected to the child by making him feel comfortable to talk about

---

33 Sunan Ibn Majah 3720, Book 33, *ḥadīth* 64. Also see, Sahih al-Bukhari 6129, Book 78, *ḥadīth* 156 and Al-Adab Al-Mufrad 384, Book 20, *ḥadīth* 13.

"Parents must be cognizant of how their actions and words can become imprinted in the minds of children."

his concerns. He was also the one who gave him the nickname Abū ʿUmayr to make him feel more mature. Naturally, children were inclined to view the Prophet ﷺ as a role model and they learned from his character and manners. They also paid attention to his gentleness as reflected in his eyes and even in the tone of his voice. The Arabs at the time were generally not very attuned to the feelings and concerns of young children, nor did they have a compassionate approach to situations such as this. However, the Prophet ﷺ did not feel the pressure to conform to this norm of tough love. The Prophet ﷺ did not dismiss Abū ʿUmayr's feelings, rather he gave him solace as he grieved over his bird. Such sensitivity and kindness should be the hallmark of every parent.

Memories

What memories have you imprinted in your children's minds?

Parents must be cognizant of how their actions and words can become imprinted in the minds of children. Something as simple as going to the mosque is a routinized part of many people's day, but what can be overlooked is that some people do not have a strong relationship with the mosque. This may be because they are young and go only occasionally to the mosque, or they may be distracted by the world outside. Often, what prevents them from going to the mosque, is those who attend it regularly.

When I was eleven years old, my father bought me a *ghuṭrah* (a traditional headdress worn by men in the Middle East). I wore it to the mosque, loving the way it made me feel. I felt like a man because my father made me feel like a man. It was Ramadan and I was excited to be in the mosque. An older man came to all the children and said, "Go to the back. Go to the back!" I looked at him, wondering if his instructions applied to me too, and he stared at me a while, wondering if I was old enough by his standards. And then he said, "Go to the back!" He made me feel afraid and insufficient. He had stripped me of the confidence I had when I had first walked into the mosque.

It is small interactions such as this that can stain children's memory and affect their relationship with their Creator.

Another vivid memory I have as a child is reading the Qur'ān once and making a mistake in my recitation. My father smiled and said to me, "You made a mistake!". My father's friend turned to me and said, "You're a champion. By Allah ﷻ, I wish my children could become like you." He made me feel amazing and I still remember it to this day. He saw value in me, despite my mistake.

It is healthy thought patterns such as these that parents need to ingrain in their children. People are more than their mistakes; they are not defined by them either. Allah ﷻ appreciates the efforts of His servants. Hence, parents must make an effort to appear welcoming and inviting to their children, especially when they express interest in their religion.

Children remember those who smile at them and those who make them feel safe. Therefore, one must extend their kindness to all of Allah's creation.

Lying to Children

I have heard the following sentiment echoed by many parents: "A little white lie here, a little white lie there; well, at least they are doing as they are told." Does lying to children even count? Many cultures would argue that it does not. Norms dictate that sometimes lying is necessary and if it leads to obedience, then there can be no harm done there. Islam, however, heavily discourages it.

Some lies are generational. They pass from one generation to another, and many individuals are not able to discern the truth. Quickly, this spirals out of control to such an extent that generations raise their children in a lineage embedded with lies. Some may think lying to children is excusable because it builds character and makes the responsibility of parenting lighter. This is lazy parenting. Children who are effectively raised on lies go on to amplify them to a greater level in their adulthood.

Some people assume that some lies are excusable for the sake of a greater good – a child being more respectful towards others or even reciting the Qur'ān more. Thus, the decision to lie may have rational grounds and apparent benefits as it may reinforce a positive behaviour. However, the roots of these lies are further lies. In effect, branches of a tree may grow exponentially, but if the roots are not sturdy, the whole tree may fall one day. Even worse is when the lies violate one's Islamic beliefs. Parents may threaten their children from a young age with Allah's anger for committing small errors, and this instils in them a sense that Allah ﷻ is unjust and harsh. They may be told lies about *Shayṭān* which can create undue fear in children.

In this manner, religion becomes a way for parents to defer their disciplinary duties and manage their children. However, it is impermissible to lie in Islam and parents cannot make up reasons for Allah's anger or tell lies about *Shayṭān* to suit their own motives. Lying cancels out the need for patiently teaching and nurturing children; it is a much easier way out.

The Prophet ﷺ stressed the importance of not lying to children. He said, "Whoever says to a child, "Come and take this," and then does not give them anything, it is considered as (one) lie."[34] Islam is sensitive to the issue of lying and this is evident in the narration about ʿAbdullāh ibn ʿAamir ؓ when he was twelve years old. He related that the Prophet ﷺ had come to his house on a visit. His mother, hoping to allow the Prophet ﷺ and the other men to have some space called him to her saying, "Can you come and give him space? I want to give you something." The Prophet ﷺ looked at her and said, "Are you really going to give him something?"

She said, "Yes."

And he said, "If you do not give him something, it would be written as a lie against you."[35]

The Prophet ﷺ acknowledged the harm of lying to children and discouraged lying even in minor situations. Lying paves the way for bigger lies and breaks trust between people. It can even lead to breaking all ties in some situations.

---

34 Ahmad and Abu Dawud 4991
35 Sahih Abu Dawud, *ḥadīth* 4991 (graded 'Hasan' by al-Albani)

Showing Kindness and Compassion to Children

It is reported that al-Ḥassan and al-Ḥusayn, the grandchildren of the Prophet ﷺ, often entered the mosque and climbed on the Prophet's back. The Companions related that, one day, they were praying behind the Prophet ﷺ when he prolonged his prostration. This went on for so long that they felt the urge to lift their heads to see if something had happened to the Prophet ﷺ. After they had finished the prayer, the Prophet ﷺ turned and said, "My grandchildren came and climbed on top of my shoulders, and I did not want to ruin their fun."[36]

The Prophet's kindness and mercy are very well-documented, and there is also evidence that this also extended to non-Muslim children. It is reported that a young Jewish boy used to serve the Prophet ﷺ and he became sick. So the Prophet ﷺ went to visit him. He sat near his head and asked him to embrace Islam. The boy looked at his father, who told him to obey Abul-Qasim and the boy embraced Islam. The Prophet ﷺ came out saying: "Praises be to Allah ﷻ Who saved the boy from the Hell fire."[37] The Prophet ﷺ did not force him to become Muslim but his compassionate treatment of the boy influenced his decision and he became Muslim.

---

36 Sahih al-Nasaa'i, *hadīth* no. 1093)
37 Sahih al-Bukhari 1356, Book 23, *hadīth* 109

HOME SWEET HOME

Having said that, showing kindness and compassion to children does not mean that discipline and correction are not necessary. The Prophet ﷺ, although known for his cheerful face, compassion and mercy, was uncompromising in the message he was sent with. He did not allow oppression to go unchallenged and was the epitome of justice. He was firm when being firm was required.

In his youth, Mu'adh ؓ would lead his people in prayer. He would recite al-Baqarah until a person left the prayer and others rebuked him saying, "Are you a hypocrite?" This led to an argument which escalated to such an extent that the matter was brought to the Prophet ﷺ about Mu'adh ؓ. There upon the Prophet ﷺ called Mu'adh ؓ and said, "Are you a troublemaker O Mu'adh ؓ! Are you a trouble maker? Recite such and such *surah's* (short ones). Do not be a cause for trouble O Mu'adh ؓ, for behind you are weak, elderly people and people with other commitments to attend to."[38]

The Prophet ﷺ wanted him to acknowledge his wrongdoing and did not just let him get away with it. Rather, he spoke to him about it and offered him a way to correct himself. Compassion is very important when dealing

---

38   Sahih al-Bukhari, 6106. Also see, Muslim 701, Sunan Abu Dawud 790 and an-Nasa'i 835

with children as they often need their parents' guidance and are keen to listen to it too.

Raising Girls

In many parts of the world, as in many cultures and homes, the desire to be blessed with baby boys is greater and stronger than the desire to be blessed with baby girls. The pride of carrying forward a family name and hopes for a greater future seems to rest, in these cultures and homes, on the shoulders of male heirs. The Prophet ﷺ encouraged Muslim to take care of their girls and not to favour boys over them. It is reported that he ﷺ said, "Whoever cares for and looks after two girls until they reach puberty, he will be with me, on the Day of Judgement, on the same plane." And he demonstrated this by joining two of his fingers together.[39]

One possible way for one to keep company with the Prophet ﷺ on the Day of Judgement is through raising the girls that Allah ﷻ has blessed them with in piety, righteousness and goodness. These girls should be protected, provided for and honoured.

Another prophetic saying states that the girls that one raises will be their protection from any punishment they

---

39   Ṣaḥīḥ Muslim, 2631.

may deserve. Their forgiveness and protection could depend on their treatment of their own daughters. However, this prophetic saying extends beyond one's daughters and includes orphaned girls who are fostered. In all cases, we are taught that we must be conscious of Allah ﷻ and develop empathy towards the girls we raise.

The Prophet ﷺ said, "Whoever has three daughters, persevered in raising them, provided food, drink and clothing for them from his own wealth, they will become a guard for him from the fire on the Day of Resurrection."[40]

The Prophet ﷺ treated his daughters – Fāṭimah, Zaynab, Umm Kulthūm and Ruqayyah ﷺ equally and, while he loved Fāṭimah ﷺ the most, he was the best father possible to all of them and did not give her any preferential treatment. Islam teaches Muslims that siblings must be treated in an equal manner, even if it accepts that one cannot control their heart or who they love more. When Fāṭimah ﷺ entered in on the Prophet ﷺ and found him sitting, he got up for her with a cheerful face, went up to her, kissed her forehead, and then made her sit in his place.[41] Compassion and

---

40 Sahih Ibn Matah, 2974
41 Jami' at-Tirmidhi 3872, Book 49, *ḥadīth* 272

kindness exuded from him effortlessly and did not obstruct his ability to be firm or set boundaries. He always made her feel valued and special. At the time of his death, the other three daughters had already passed on, and he had buried and grieved over them all. Fāṭimah ﷺ, who was the youngest and was used to her father standing for her whenever she visited him, even when he was sick, realized that his last illness was serious when he did not greet her in his usual way. She fell to the ground crying saying, "Father, are you going through immense pain?" He replied, "Yes, it is fine; there will be no more pain for your father after this day."

He sought to console her and dispel her worries even in this condition. He did not dismiss her feelings, but he acknowledged that his pain aggrieved her. It is this emotional intelligence and how he dealt with the situation he was in that we must pay attention to. His compassion was not just reserved for those outside his home and, even in his most vulnerable state, he knew how to reassure his daughter. Through his example, we learn what it means to be a parent.

It is also important that the women of any household feel empowered to speak up and share their thoughts and opinions. When the Prophet ﷺ intended to marry any of his daughters to someone, he asked her if this is what she really wanted. He arranged the marriage of ʿAlī ؓ to his most beloved Fāṭimah ؓ and he married two of his daughters to ʿUthmān ibn ʿAffān ؓ and his daughter Zaynab ؓ to a man who reverted to Islam late. Through these examples, we see how the Prophet ﷺ did not impose his will, and actively created an environment wherein his daughters felt they could freely share their thoughts.

Parents & Relatives

Do you remember to thank your parents and remember them in your duʿā's?

Do you reflect on your parenting methods?

The Rights of Parents

Allah ﷻ said in *Sūrah Luqmān*,

وَوَصَّيْنَا الْإِنسَانَ بِوَالِدَيْهِ حَمَلَتْهُ أُمُّهُ وَهْنًا عَلَىٰ وَهْنٍ وَفِصَالُهُ فِي عَامَيْنِ أَنِ اشْكُرْ لِي وَلِوَالِدَيْكَ إِلَيَّ الْمَصِيرُ وَإِن جَاهَدَاكَ عَلَىٰ أَن تُشْرِكَ بِي مَا لَيْسَ لَكَ بِهِ عِلْمٌ فَلَا تُطِعْهُمَا وَصَاحِبْهُمَا فِي الدُّنْيَا مَعْرُوفًا وَاتَّبِعْ سَبِيلَ مَنْ أَنَابَ إِلَيَّ ثُمَّ إِلَيَّ مَرْجِعُكُمْ فَأُنَبِّئُكُم بِمَا كُنتُمْ تَعْمَلُونَ

We enjoined upon man to be dutiful to his parents. His mother bore him in weakness upon weakness, and his weaning lasted two years. (We, therefore, enjoined upon him): "Give thanks to Me and to your parents. To Me is your ultimate return. But if they press you to associate others with Me in My Divinity, (to associate) those regarding whom you have no knowledge (that they are My associates), do not obey them.[42]

---

42 Surah Luqmān 31: 14–15

HOME SWEET HOME

Allah ﷻ commands children to honour their parents and reflect on the hardships they endure for their sake. The mother is given the highest honours due to the immense pain and difficulties she goes through while bringing up her children. Although we are taught to listen to our parents and be courteous to them, Allah ﷻ sets clear the firm parameters of *ḥalāl* and *ḥarām*. Therefore, children's obedience to Allah ﷻ takes precedence over their obedience to their parents if the instructions conflict. If parents are disbelievers and use their position to influence their children to disobey Allah ﷻ, these verses empower and reassure them that they do not have to obey them. Following the advice of one's parents should not be to the detriment of their faith. Instead, one is commanded to conform to Islamic principles and teachings. We are reminded that our lives are always under the command of Allah ﷻ and that everything happens according to His plan. Ultimately, we will all return to Him and must be prepared to give an account of our deeds and actions. Living our lives in accordance with His laws and reminding ourselves that we will be judged for our words and deeds, encourage us to live a better life.

On the Day of Judgement, none shall escape Allah's judgement. Incorrectly, one may assume that one can delude themselves with entertainment and trivial matters. But on that Day, no one will escape reckoning regarding how they have dealt with the rights of others. On that day, the truth will be revealed.

Allah ﷻ will ask us about our duty towards our parents. Parents and their children have a duty towards each other, but we will be questioned about our role specifically. Allah ﷻ clearly states that we must fulfil our duty towards our parents, but are not obliged to obey them in the disobedience of Allah ﷻ. Moreover, their obedience regarding other matters is also not absolute. The word used in the Qur'ān and *ḥadīth* for dutifulness towards parents is *birr*, which means kindness, courtesy and goodness. There is no verse in the Qur'ān which says we must obey our parents in absolute terms. However, parents do have rights upon their children and their shortcomings deserve to be overlooked. They also deserve to be defended and protected by their children to the best of their ability. Among the definitions of *birr* towards one's parents is that a child should not raise their voice above theirs, even if they have raised theirs first. Allah ﷻ will judge them for their actions. In some cases, they may even have the right to do so if there is a good reason for it. It is not up to us to make judgements about their actions. Our duty towards them is simply not to raise our voice at them. When shouting at one's parents becomes a key characteristic of someone's personality, in all likelihood, this will be mirrored in their relationship with their children and the cycle will repeat itself.

Our best efforts may fall short of expectations, but Allah ﷻ sees our efforts. The worldviews of parents and their children may be so polarized that both believe that the other's way of thinking is unfathomable. Sometimes, parents can be clearly wrong. The time and generation in which they grew up in is different from their children's time and generation, and so dissonance between parents and their children is expected.

Despite this expectation, one does not have the right to hurt their parents with their words or actions. Part of being kind and dutiful to one's parents is to give them advice and guidance in a beautiful and acceptable manner. As the example of the Prophet ﷺ shows, it is permissible and encouraged to be firm when setting expectations. One must be uncompromising in relation to Islamic values, but this must be conveyed in a kind and sincere way. We should advise our parents to avoid any sinful behaviour out of love for them and desire to help them because we want to save them from Allah's anger and the Hellfire.

In *Sūrah Maryam*, Allah ﷻ relates Prophet Ibrāhīm's ﷺ concern for his father. Prophet Ibrāhīm ﷺ is mentioned in numerous instances in the Qur'ān advising his father.

PARENTS & RELATIVES

His love, mercy and concern for his father extended beyond this world and included the Hereafter. Without showing any disrespect for his father, Ibrāhīm ﷺ warned him against inclining to the evil *Shayṭān* and criticized the idol worship prevalent around him. He used the knowledge Allah ﷻ bestowed on him honourably to save him from his errors.

Additionally, our respect for our parents extends beyond mere interactions with them. The Prophet ﷺ said, "Verily, among the major sins is that a man curses his own parents." It was said, "O Messenger of Allah ﷺ, how can a man curse his own parents?" The Prophet ﷺ said, "He insults the father of another man, and then that man insults his father and his mother."[43]

Moreover, one is taught that saying 'fie!' to their parents is forbidden. Victimhood mentality may lead one to focus only on the wrongs committed by others and potentially justify retaliation against them, which is not permissible in Islam. The justification may begin with "Oh, but they..." as if it is enough to warrant whatever unlawful action that follows. It may be that a wrong has been committed against them. Undoubtedly, Allah ﷻ sees that and will judge that action according to His justice and wisdom. It is important that we will all be

---

[43] Ṣaḥīḥ al-Bukhari 5973, Ṣaḥīḥ Muslim 90

held responsible for wronging others, particularly our parents. It is much easier to wrong our parents or those closest to us and those who have witnessed our every fall and rise. However, for the sake of our development and to maintain our honour, personal issues with parents and those closest to us must be addressed. A victimhood mentality only leads to more victims. Individuals who feel victimized suffer in multiple ways, most importantly because they have unaddressed traumas. If unresolved, this cycle will continue. By criticizing and blaming the other person with whom one is in conflict, it becomes very difficult to find a solution. If such is the course of action, one deflects all blame towards others and takes no responsibility for their own actions. For the betterment of oneself and those around them, this negative attitude needs to be dealt with. One deserves to be a respectful individual who frees themselves from the unlawful fetters of blaming others. One deserves to be happy as well as a dignified individual. Therefore, one must take responsibility to grow out of this negative cycle and break out of it once and for all. Such bad traits are not genetically programmed but socially taught and retaught as one generation succeeds another. Allah ﷻ will hold every single person responsible for the wrongs they commit.

PARENTS & RELATIVES

Obligations

Parents have a right to be obeyed and respected by their children. However, there are three situations where one is not obligated to obey their parents.

The first is if it means disobedience to Allah ﷻ. For example, this would involve any commands which would hinder or stop their ability to conduct obligatory religious practices, ordering them to steal or cheat, cutting off their siblings and other family ties, facilitating a forbidden transaction or forbidden service, bearing false witness and ordering them to purchase alcohol, pork or recreational drugs.

The second situation is if the parents' request does not concern them and has no beneficial or harmful implications for them on a personal level. For example, this might be pushing their child to study a specific course, buying a particular brand of car, working a specific job, marrying a person of their choice, ordering them to ask their wife to work, demanding that their grandchildren go to a specific school and making them use their own money to pay or gift a person of their choice.

Imam Malik ؒ narrated, "A married man said to me that whenever I get a gift/wage, my mother tells me I must give from it to my sister first, before anyone else."

Imam Malik ﷺ replied, "That is not an obligation upon you to obey your mother in this matter, but maintain respect and kindness to your mother in how you deal with the matter."

The third situation is if the parents ask them to obey them in a matter which violates their own rights or the rights of others. This may be if a child is physically unable to carry out the duty or if it will cause them harm. Other examples include, ordering one's child to surrender their wages to them, coercing their daughter to give them her *Mahar* or taking it without her permission, telling their child to drive faster than the speed limit or obligating them to give up their car when they have a need for it, walking in the heat or cold unnecessarily, obligating the son to make his wife live with her in-laws, making his wife spend money on her in-laws and commanding their child to undergo an unnecessary medical or traditional health procedure.

It is to be strictly noted that although the above religious principles are true, the son or daughter must maintain respect and kindness to their parents, even if they do not carry out their parents' request.

The son and daughter must always monitor their language and actions towards their parents, regardless of whether their request is right or wrong, and must never respond in a hurtful way towards them in any circumstance.

Furthermore, concerns and confusions regarding monetary obligations are often key causes of conflict in parent-child relationships. Whilst in Islam financial obligations are primarily on the male children, there can be some circumstances which mean that the daughter also becomes financially obligated to her parents. There is an expectation that a son financially helps his parents if he is financially independent and can afford to do so. For a daughter, this expectation is set if there is an absence of sons and if her parents are struggling with basic needs and she can afford to help them.

Emphasis is put on the son to assist his parents if they are in financial need or if their money/property is not sufficient to cover their day-to-day needs such as clothing, shelter, food and necessary bills. It is imperative this does not lead to him neglecting his wife and children in the process. In addition, a man should not obligate his wife to work so that they can cover the expenses of his parents and relatives. Neither is it permissible to take her wealth and send it to them. Furthermore, the wife should not place restrictions on who her husband supports, especially if they have been sufficiently financially provided for by him. They must not issue unrealistic demands or issue ultimatums without a valid reason. Our Islamic principles should help us falling into extremes, causing neglect or violating rights and obligations. May Allah ﷻ grant us ease and foresight in all matters.

Moreover, if the parents are not in any financial need, then the son is not obligated to spend on them beyond what he chooses out of the kindness and goodness of his heart according to what he can afford. It is a clear violation of a child's right if the parents have enough money and yet demand their children to give them a monthly allowance. Despite not having to obey this request, it is paramount that this matter is dealt with in a way that maintains respect and kindness. In the event that the child chooses to give money and helps settle any potential conflict, they will be rewarded by Allah ﷻ.

In a very small number of cases, it is permissible for parents to take from their child's property and money without their permission. However, there are four very strict conditions which must be established beforehand.

The first condition is that there should be a dire need for it such as, paying a bill or buying food. This is evidenced in *Al-Hakim* and authenticated by *Albani*.

$$\text{إنَّ أولادَكم هِبَةُ اللهِ لكم يَهَبُ لمن يشاءُ إناثًا ويَهبُ لمن يشاءُ الذُّكورَ، فهم و أموالُهم لكم إذا احتجتُم (رواه الحاكم وصححه الالباني) إليها}$$

'Your children are a gift from Allah ﷻ to you, He gifts to whomever He wills - daughters or sons. They and their wealth and property are permissible for you if you are in need.'

The above *ḥadīth* clarifies the misconception that a child and their wealth and property all belong to their father. Some falsely claim this by referring to another authentic *ḥadīth* 'You and your wealth belongs to your father'

$$\text{- أنت ومالك لأبيك.}$$

(Ibn Majah, Abu Dawud, Ahmed).

Jurists and all schools of thought unanimously agree that this is not a literal statement and that it means, it is 'permissible' for the father to use some of his child's wealth to support his living necessities if the father does not have enough to support himself and his child's mother. The *ḥadīth* does not mean that the father 'owns' his child and their wealth and property, otherwise the father would be entitled to inherit his child's entire wealth. Rather, it is established in the Qur'an that the inheritance is divided between different heirs after death. The mother is not mentioned in the *ḥadīth* because it is a given that the father is responsible for the mother (except if the mother is widowed, in which case she has the same right as the father).

The second condition is that the amount the parents need will not cause harm to their child. For example, by taking money from their son, the son can no longer pay his own bills.

The third condition is that the amount of money or property the parents need does not impact the child's livelihood. For example, by taking their child's car during the time they need to commute to work.

The fourth condition is that the money and property taken is not given to their siblings or other people without their permission.

The above situations are unanimously agreed upon principles among the jurists. However, as an act of kindness or goodness, it is recommended that children are generous to their parents whenever they can afford to do so.

Regarding the debts of parents, one must remember that regardless of whether the parents are alive or not, children are not obligated to pay off their debts. Therefore, in the event of their demise, Islam has dictated that debts should be settled from any wealth or property they have leftover before inheritance is distributed.

PARENTS & RELATIVES

Advice and Reflection

The following are general advisory points for children to reflect on regarding their relationship with their parents.

1. Acknowledge, validate, tell and thank them often;
2. Mention and conduct random acts of appreciation;
3. Sporting spirit by being uplifting and encouraging;
4. Avoid their bad and connect through the good;
5. Learn their moods and values;
6. Ask advice from experienced and trusted people.

The following are general advisory points for parents to reflect on regarding their relationship with their children, especially as they move from childhood to adolescence.

1. Listen; be non-judgemental;
2. Show interest in their hobbies;
3. Talk about one's feelings;
4. Acknowledge, validate, tell and thank them often;
5. Give space; let go of control;
6. Agree together on rules; give and take;
7. Set boundaries under your roof.

The following are general advisory points for children to reflect on when dealing with a strained relationship with their parents.

1. Stay calm;
2. Manage the situation as best as you can; do not try forcing them to change;
3. Do not retaliate by arguing and disregard any attempts of denigration;
4. Look to your future for hope;
5. Make *du'ā'* to guide them. Believe in yourself after Allah ﷻ;
6. Talk to someone you trust;
7. Look after yourself.

PARENTS & RELATIVES

The Forgotten Years

From a foetus in the womb to a wholly dependent baby, from a curious toddler to a child who thinks they do not need their parents, and finally to an adult who does not need his or her parents but wants them all the same – our life evolves from being completely dependent on our parents to fully independent individuals. It is easy to overlook the years when one has no memory of. So, when our parents' eyes twinkle with joy and glisten over with the years of our childhood, it is easy for us to feel completely detached. One story after another: how we tripped and fell; how the pigeons reacted when we ran towards them; or the time our laughter rang loudly in the quiet train. We have heard it all before and it was not exciting after the first time.

These stories do not have the same nostalgic effect on us. The people in these stories may seem to be just characters in a novel and do not exactly match the parents presently in front of us; not the ones who have grown old and weary, or the ones from our childhood memories. Some memories may still be there, but if they are not, it is important to pinpoint where the gap between us and our parents began and the reasons for it, and then try to bridge that gap. Sometimes in the hustle and bustle of life, or due to cultural norms, parental love may not be expressed aptly. The traumas the parents may have suffered, and their insecurities and other issues can create a strain on their relationship with their children.

Exhaustive efforts must be exercised to relieve this strain and ensure this does not repeat itself with the next generation.

The Prophet ﷺ said, "Your mother, your mother, your mother, and then your father."[44] The honourable status of the mother is incomparable and incontestable. The scholars state that one owes their mother the most – three times more than they owe to their father. In particular, Islam raises the honour of the mother as she is the one who carried the child for nine months. The constraints the mother is subjected to in those nine months, the difficulties she faces, and the love and care she devotes to the development and growth of her baby, make her deserving of that honourable status. The second reason for her special honourable status is the labour she endures and how she suffers as she brings her child into the world in unimaginable pain while subjecting herself to serious risks. The third reason is she may face challenges and difficulties when providing essential nourishment to her newborn through breastfeeding, as well as being the

---

44   Sahih Muslim, Book 32, no. 6181

nourishment and strength for the child. Her honourable status is not limited to these three reasons, but each of these reasons is immensely significant and rewarding. Therefore, the gratitude one owes to their mother cannot be measured. None of these three reasons applies to the father and this is what discerns the honourable status of mothers in Islam. Some fathers may initially find it hard to forge an emotional connection with their baby. In some cases, the desire to protect and provide may be there immediately; in other cases, it will require patience and perseverance for these bonds to develop and grow over time

Both parents must ensure that they provide a stable environment for their baby. If either of them, or both, struggle with mental health, then assistance must be sought.

Apart from the initial carrying of the baby, labour and breastfeeding, both parents have equal responsibilities and duties towards raising their children, and so they deserve to be treated equally by their children. Children must strive to balance their treatments of both parents, despite perhaps loving one of them more than the other– something acknowledged in Islam as out of one's control.

To Be the Change One Wants to See

The home environment heavily impacts children's development as it is the first learning environment they encounter. The norms and values the children learn in their initial socialization at home set them up for the world. This initial preparation at home should prepare and aid them in their interactions outside the home.

Similarly, children look up to their parents and adopt their norms and values, which means that parents should also understand that they can also learn from their children. As children belong to a new generation, their world looks different and sharing their experiences with their parents should be seen by the latter as a learning opportunity. Perhaps they have more educational or career opportunities than their parents ever imagined possible, and so listening to them means that parents can also benefit from them. With open communication and dialogue, the worlds that separate parents from their children can come together, and better understanding between them can be achieved.

The catalyst for change is not always someone who is older, but one who has stronger faith (*imān*) – even if they have less knowledge. Children, even adult children, may not always have the ability to intervene and

"With open communication and dialogue, the worlds that separate parents from their children can come together."

change lifelong misguided beliefs, but Allah ﷻ has made supplication (*duʿāʾ*) to Him accessible to all and did not limit it to people of a certain age or a geographical location. One is taught to use supplication to connect with Allah ﷻ and ask Him for forgiveness, express their gratitude to Him and ask for their needs and wishes. Allah ﷻ hears all the *duʿāʾs* raised to Him.

One must make *duʿāʾ* for their parents and children. We are taught that a parent's *duʿāʾ* for their children is answered and so we must ensure that our parents always pray for us and that we always pray for our parents. We should pray for what is advantageous to them. Sometimes, it is difficult to help family members who are not ready to accept help yet. For them, we should continue to pray for their guidance and healing.

Trying to tackle issues one may face with their parents who violate Islamic principles can take a great deal of time and effort. In such cases, it is important to be patient with them, in the way the parents would have shown one patience before. There should be no expectation that they will change straightaway. One's effort is seen by Allah ﷻ and He does not let any good deed or word go to waste.

Expressing curiosity is one way of strengthening the relationship between a parent and their child. In addition, learning about the barriers to their engagement with Islamic principles can better inform decisions and actions taken forward.

Children grow up and navigate the world, often in territories not familiar to their parents. It is the same world, yet so different. One must not forget that despite the differences, parental advice can still be very useful. Even if many things have stayed and will stay the same, asking one's parents for advice is always important. Their experiences and insights about the world can be combined with the children's own experiences and insights. One should also include them in their decisions even if they disagree with them. For even if they do not think the final decision is the best course of action, at least the journey to the decision was made with them. Ignorance and egos may come between children and parents, thus destroying this channel of communication. Therefore, both parents and children must struggle against their own egos and educate themselves.

However, some situations are too extreme to be dealt with directly and external help should be sought. These exceptional situations should be acknowledged, and matters examined on a case-by-case basis. If the situation is extreme, it is strongly recommended that children do not just rely on the above methods, but strive to find the best help they can. For all other cases that fall under the 'norm', parents deserve to have their rights from their children. A duty to honour these rights should be present in all children who have parents who took care of them and raised them well.

Maintaining Courteous Relationships

Like many companions, Asmā' ﷺ, the daughter of Abū Bakr al-Ṣiddīq ﷺ, appreciated the wisdom and knowledge of the Prophet ﷺ. One day, she went to the Prophet ﷺ and said about her mother, "O Messenger of Allah ﷺ, she is a non-Muslim and she hates Islam. She wants to visit me and has a gift for me. Should I allow her to visit me and can I accept her gift?"

The Prophet ﷺ said, "Yes, keep your ties with your mother and accept the gift."[45]

Throughout history, Muslims have always worried about their relationship with non-Muslim family members. Narrations like the above one serve as a reminder that, even when there are religious differences, ties of kinship must still be maintained. In the case of Asmā' ﷺ, her mother tried to be courteous to her, and she reciprocated this by being welcoming and courteous to her mother. New Muslims may face tension and strain in

---

45   Sahih al-Bukhari 2620 and Muslim 1003 (Arabic version)

PARENTS & RELATIVES

their family relationships, especially if some members have a particular aversion to Islam. In such situations, the new Muslim must do their duty and keep ties to the best of their ability. This is a great test, and it requires patience and resilience. The new Muslim's love for Islam may end up drawing their parents to it too. *Duʿāʾ*'s are heard by the One who has power over all things. Hence, the new Muslim should not despair, instead they must strengthen their relationship with Allah ﷻ. Over time, witnessing the positive transformation on their son or daughter may quell the parents' fears and improve their relationship with their new Muslim son or daughter.

While the Prophet ﷺ did not get to see his father, who died before he was born, it is well documented how he honoured and respected his father's brothers, his father's friends, those who were Muslim and those who were non-Muslim. He used to say, "Respecting your uncle is like respecting your father."[46] Through his example, we see how he respected his uncle Ḥamzah ؓ before and after he accepted Islam. He respected Abū Ṭālib even though he never became a Muslim. He was also always incredibly respectful to his uncle Abu Lahab who was a hostile enemy of Islam to such an extent that he was cursed by Allah ﷻ in the Qur'ān.

---

[46] Sahih Abu Dawud 1623

HOME SWEET HOME

Allah ﷻ, Mighty and Majestic, said,

$$تَبَّتْ يَدَا أَبِي لَهَبٍ وَتَبَّ$$

Destroyed were the hands of Abū Lahab, and he lay utterly doomed.[47]

This was because he put fire in front of the Prophet ﷺ, worked against him and declared his enmity against him. Yet, before Islam, Abū Lahab had loved the Prophet ﷺ and had two of his sons engaged to two of the daughters of the Prophet ﷺ. After the Prophet ﷺ proclaimed his mission, Abū Lahab annulled the engagement and made public his hatred of Islam and his nephew. Despite the barrage of insults and harm he faced from his uncle Abū Lahab, the Prophet ﷺ continued to show him respect and never retaliated against him.

The Prophet ﷺ shone through all these challenges. He was a family man who served his family and relatives and loved to do so; he cared for them deeply and they reciprocated this by caring about him and respecting him.

Another *ḥadīth* shows how he honoured his parents even in their deaths. One day, 'Umar ﷺ, along with some other companions, saw the Prophet ﷺ on his knees at a grave crying profusely. They said to him, "What is making you cry so we might cry with you?" "This is

---

47   Surah al-Lahab 111: 1

the grave of the mother of your Prophet," he replied. She had died when the Prophet ﷺ was six years old. This shows that the intensity of his love for his mother had never diminished. In another narration, he said, "Allah ﷻ did not allow me to make istighfar for her, so tenderness struck me like the tenderness a child feels to his parent."[48]

Like the Prophet ﷺ, we are also likely to have happy memories of our childhood with our parents. We owe them for those memories and, if in some cases, anyone has been harmed by them, then it is best that they avoid ruminating over these memories alone. In such cases, it is important to seek outside help. We are taught to treat our relatives kindly and, even if they mistreat us, we are taught not to mistreat them. The Prophet ﷺ advised against reacting against bad manners with bad manners and encouraged opting for goodness instead.

Allah ﷻ says,

$$\text{وَبَيْنَهُ عَدَاوَةٌ كَأَنَّهُ وَلِيٌّ حَمِيمٌ}$$

'…*respond to evil with what is best, then the one you are in a feud with will be like a close friend*'[49]

Maintaining a distance vis-à-vis one's parents or other

---
48   Ibn Habban 986
49   Surah Fussilat 41: 34

family members may be necessary for the sake of one's sanity and health. However, even in such a case, the principle of maintaining a courteous relationship still applies. Therefore, only pleasant words should be exchanged and all encounters should be kept civil and polite.

In the event that distance between family members is needed, it should be done in a way that allows for respect and dignity to remain.

Showing Concern for One's Relatives

The Prophet's courtesy is ubiquitous in the *Sīrah*. He once said to his companions, "You will soon conquer Egypt where al-Qirat is frequently mentioned. So when you conquer it, treat its inhabitants well. For there lies upon you the responsibility because of blood ties or relationship [with them]."[50] The Prophet ﷺ was speaking of a blood relationship that went back 4,000 years and he still used this connection to show how he honoured his lineage. The Muslims eventually entered Egypt during the time of Abū Bakr ؓ with ʿAmr ibn al-ʿĀṣ ؓ, so he had forewarned them about how they should conduct themselves. The Prophet ﷺ

---

50 Sahih Muslim in Riyad as-Salihin 328. Note: the 'blood ties' or 'kinship' in this *ḥadīth* are referring to Hajar's mother, who is the ancestral father of the Quraish pope (i.e. the prophet ﷺ) and a relationship with Mariyah, the Copt, the mother of Ibrahim, who is the son of Prophet Muhammed ﷺ.

often referred to the Egyptians as his in-laws due to his relationship with Mariyah al-Qibṭiyyah ﷺ who came from the Copts of Egypt.

His concern for his family is evident from his first call to Islam. Before calling the world to Islam, he first called his own family to Islam. Allah ﷻ instructed him in the Qur'ān,

$$وَأَنذِرْ عَشِيرَتَكَ الْأَقْرَبِينَ$$

And warn your nearest kinsmen; [51]

He was told that he must warn and save those closest to him. Some of them heeded the message whilst others rejected it. Some were amongst the staunchest enemies of Islam. Despite this, the Prophet ﷺ did not give up on them; he just avoided their mistreatment and connected warmly to those relatives who still loved him and around whom he felt safe.

In particular, the Prophet ﷺ loved and respected his uncle al-ʿAbbās ﷺ and maintained a good relationship with him. During the Battle of Badr, the Prophet's uncle al-ʿAbbās, who was still a non-Muslim at the time, was

---

51 Surah al-Shuʿarā' 26: 214

HOME SWEET HOME

captured as a prisoner of war. He was tied up so firmly that the Prophet ﷺ heard his moaning due to the pain he felt. The companions, ever attentive to the Prophet ﷺ, said, "O Messenger of Allah ﷺ, we see that you look uncomfortable and distressed."

In response, the Prophet ﷺ said, "I can hear my uncle's moaning." Upon hearing this, one of the companions, who had brought him in as a war prisoner, untied his shackles and the moaning stopped. He said to the Prophet ﷺ, "O Messenger of Allah ﷺ, I saw your distress, and for your sake – because he is your uncle - I untied his shackles."

The Prophet ﷺ thanked him for his leniency but recognized the potential harm of preferential treatment and that disparity in the treatment of prisoners of war was a form of injustice, and so, he ordered him, "Now, go back to the other prisoners and untie their shackles."[52]

Later on, al-ʿAbbās became a Muslim and reflected on the kindness his nephew had shown him, even though they had just met on the battlefield as opponents. It is in such moments that the Prophet ﷺ naturally attracted people to Islam.

---

52 al-Baihaqy in Sunan al-Kubra (9/89) no. 17924, Book of Biographies, under 'The Prisoner is to be Shackled'.

This anecdote not only shows the compassion of the Prophet ﷺ towards his relatives and his strong sense of justice, but also his understanding that just as the cries of his uncle pained him, his visible distress also pained his companions. Their mutual love meant that a middle ground needed to be found where all these factors were taken into consideration.

Here, we see evidence of the Prophet's ﷺ attentiveness and awareness of the ripple effects of his actions. A quality that we observe throughout his *sīrah*.

Spouses

How can we balance our relationships?

How can one please their spouse, parents and in-laws?

The Importance of Marriage

Marriage is an act of worship. Allah ﷻ rewards for marriage as He rewards for other acts of worship. Marriage can be a pathway to Paradise, but like with all other blessings, it can also come with great tests. Marriage is more than just infatuation or love. One should engage in a period of deep thinking and reflection before getting married. One must be careful that they do not view marriage as a tick-box exercise or just a way to fulfil their physical desire. The Prophet ﷺ encouraged young people to get married. He said,

SPOUSES

$$\text{يَا مَعْشَرَ الشَّبَابِ مَنِ اسْتَطَاعَ مِنْكُمُ الْبَاءَةَ فَلْيَتَزَوَّجْ}$$

O young men [and O young women], whoever among you can afford it, let him get married.[53]

In the Qur'ān, Allah ﷻ, Mighty and Majestic, says,

$$\text{وَأَنكِحُوا الْأَيَامَىٰ مِنكُمْ وَالصَّالِحِينَ مِنْ عِبَادِكُمْ وَإِمَائِكُمْ}$$
$$\text{إِن يَكُونُوا فُقَرَاءَ يُغْنِهِمُ اللَّهُ مِن فَضْلِهِ ۗ وَاللَّهُ وَاسِعٌ عَلِيمٌ}$$

Marry those of you that are single, (whether men or women), and those of your male and female slaves that are righteous. If they are poor, Allah will enrich them out of His Bounty. Allah is Immensely Resourceful, All-Knowing.[54]

Allah ﷻ promises that He will assist them by providing and supporting them. Throughout the Qur'ān and *Sunnah*, marriage is given importance and an honourable status. Marriage is encouraged especially for the man if he can afford to provide for a wife and children. Communities are responsible for facilitating marriages and making the process smooth by giving support to those who are single. If those seeking marriage are financially poor, Allah ﷻ promises to assist them by providing for them and supporting them. Allah ﷻ also gives responsibility to the community and the parents

---

53 Sunan an-Nasa'I 3209, Book 26, *ḥadīth* 14. Also see, Vol. 4, Book 26, *ḥadīth* 3211.
54 Surah al-Nūr 24: 32

to support their children to get married when they are ready to do so.

The binding force of marriage is taken very seriously in the Qur'ān. It is called,

$$\text{مِيثَاقًا غَلِيظًا}$$

a firm covenant [55]

It is a promise and sealed agreement between the married couple - a firm covenant of fidelity. With this covenant comes rights and responsibilities and the promise of love, support and help between the spouses. As couples grow together and have children, the marriage promise they made to each other entails raising their children under the guidance sent by Allah ﷻ. They have to do their utmost best to harmoniously uphold the rights of Allah ﷻ in the home. The new couple should fear Allah ﷻ regarding the covenant they have made.

Parental and Societal Influence on Marriage

In a hyper-sexualized society, where temptations and desires are not confined to outside one's home but also pervade phone and TV screens, the institution of marriage is constantly questioned and under threat.

---

[55] Surah al-Nisā' 4: 21

SPOUSES

Oftentimes, marriage is delayed because there is a lack of support for it.

It may be the case that a man or a woman is ready for marriage, and has independent financial stability, but they are discouraged from getting married because they are in their early twenties and still in some form of education or training. They are, on the one hand, strongly advised against pursuing an unlawful relationship, but on the other hand, they are offered no support to pursue marriage, despite marriage being a very attractive objective which they should aspire to. Hence, in this situation, they have no other option but to control their desires and temptations. Unfortunately, the sad reality is that in this day and age, pursuing marriage is an arduous and lengthy process, filled with obstacles, ego and pride.

Young men and women are told to control their desires and temptations while at the same time still maintain a positive outlook on marriage. Fasting is presented as a viable option to curb their desires and silence any further discussion. These young men and women are taught to stay away from illicit sex and control their temptations. When marriage is brought up, they themselves may struggle to be on board with such a serious commitment. Parents sometimes become consumed with their own personal desires, needs and concerns over how they will be perceived by their community. Some parents act as if they are the ones who have the decision to make the prayer of seeking guidance (*istikhārah*) again and again and then go to their children saying that Allah ﷻ has shown them that a certain girl or boy is not good for them. This is pure selfishness and ignorance. One cannot pray the prayer of guidance for someone else. The one who should make it is the one who is getting married.

Interferences like this make marriage difficult and a battlefield for the family. Whereas Islam is simple and straightforward when it comes to marriage. Islam teaches that marriage should be facilitated and made easy.

Discussing 'Taboo' Topics

Parents should open the door for discussions around marriage and relationships. Many subtopics under these might be seen as sensitive and be uncomfortable to speak about. Despite this, we should not shy away from discussing them or even classify them as 'taboo' topics. There are over 3,000 questions in the books of fiqh about sexuality – how then can one make it a taboo topic? Children will inevitably pick things up from the outside world and, when they have questions, they should be able to freely speak about them with their parents. Otherwise, they will find other outlets to discuss or express their natural needs in ways that may be inappropriate. These discussions would be ideally opened and started before they start discovering their attraction to the opposite sex. Parents should be supportive and encourage their children to make decisions in their best interests. Recognizing changes in their children due to their developmental growth will help create a greater sense of understanding with them. Parents should lift and boost their children's self-esteem and remind them that societal judgement is ever-changing, and perceptions of beauty are superficial. They should also remind them that flaunting themselves on social media for the sake of a dopamine rush is not worth the sins they will incur as a result. Young men and women do not push boundaries because they want to bring Allah's wrath and anger on them, but because society makes them question their own worth and value.

In the murky world of pornography, it is more common for women and girls to be the objectified products and men the consumers, but nowadays it is evident that human bodies, regardless of gender, are objectified and sexualized ubiquitously. As a consequence, discussions around prohibitions and respect need to be held in the home.

Due to the stigma attached to certain topics, prolific sex crimes go unpunished because the victims are afraid to speak out for fear of judgement and dismissal. Through sexual abuse, prostitution and trafficking, the mass exploitation of women continues. A big contributing factor is that communities, especially Muslim communities, are yet to overcome their unwarranted feelings of shame and embarrassment. They close their eyes when unwanted or unexpected pregnancies and abortions happen. But even when this has not happened, discussions about it are closed from the onset.

Parents protest when schools bring up topics about sexuality, sex crimes, pregnancies and sex education but, at the same time, they are not willing to open the discussion up themselves. Children will somehow learn about these things naturally, but they also need their parents' guidance and support. Without opening this discussion with their parents, children may not be fully equipped to deal with the challenges that society throws at them.

Young people should also be confident when they approach their parents about these issues and break the taboo barrier. Open conversations are valuable to their relationship with their parents and their understanding of each other.

Discussions before Marriage

Addictions, health issues, debts and financial constraints, among other issues, should be discussed before marriage so that one can make an informed decision before

"Parents should lift and boost their children's self-esteem and remind them that societal judgement is ever-changing, and perceptions of beauty are superficial."

accepting a proposal. Discussing these matters is of paramount importance. Marrying someone without first addressing any issues (if present) is a form of dishonesty.

Modern society conditions young men and women to believe that delaying their marriage is necessary for the betterment of their future. Men are told they need to finish their degrees, become stable in their jobs, and only when they have become secure in their careers, should they consider marriage. Objectively, this is not bad advice. It is only when the requirements keep piling up. Some parents may turn down proposals for their daughters from young men who do not fit their ideal in terms of education and status.

As a result, these same men may succumb to alternative and illicit ways to satisfy their desires. They may even question why they should restrict themselves to a contractually binding relationship. Blocking the path to marriage or overly complicating it can lead to drastic social consequences.

The above may also apply to women, who are judged even more harshly by society for the same transgressions. From a young age, girls are made to dream about their wedding day: the happy-ever-after moment. This is the image they are sold in terms of marriage. However, when they get older, they learn that marriage is far from the fantasy they have been sold. They find out that the men around them are not like the men they have read about in books. In fact, the horrors of the reality of the world comes at them in their first few years of life. Asking any woman about when she first felt unequal to men, harassed by a man or made to feel like an object will explain why so many women have a sense of mistrust towards men. This sense of mistrust is not necessarily an aversion to men, but it is a defensive reaction to protect themselves from being exploited and taken advantage of.

Women should be taught from a young age to be confident and have love for themselves so they do not fall prey to the harm around them. Yet, it seems that, in many cases, no preventative measures could have stopped the harm that they would go on to face. As a result, there is benefit when women wait until they feel confident, independent and ready before they decide to get married. However, sometimes society exploits this by presenting marriage and having children as a restrictive, career-sabotaging institution. Marriage and children are not synonymous with failure to combat hegemonic ideals, yet this is how society presents it.

Society teaches that a woman's independence is tied to her views on marriage and that a strong woman must be dedicated to her professional career after completing her higher education. If she fails to do so, she will miss the golden years of her life because of patriarchal ideals. Such views do not even consider the argument that marriage does not have to come at the cost of a successful professional career. It is almost as if a woman must choose between either a successful professional career or a successful marriage. Put under such terms, the professional career may take precedence and marriage is therefore delayed. Deep down, modern society devalues femininity and motherhood, presenting them as hindrances to a successful career and personal independence. As a result, women nowadays are delaying having children and consequently many women struggle to get pregnant after they have passed their peak period of fertility.

Islam teaches that both men and women have a right to be educated and to have a career, but it also teaches us the importance of marriage and having a family. Islam values motherhood and marriage and actively encourages both. A balanced approach is needed and to do this, one must examine their priorities in life and realign them with the teachings of Islam. Women and men must all look to Islam as the solution.

What Does One's Spouse Love?

Gary Chapman in his book, *The Five Love Languages: How to Express Heartfelt Commitment to Your Mate*, speaks of the importance of learning the way one's partner feels loved. The five love languages: acts of service, receiving gifts, quality time, words of affirmation and physical touch are all alluded to in the above book.[56] Becoming more attuned to one's partner's needs strengthens the marriage and makes it more fulfilling. The table below is from decades of research by Muslim experts and judges.[57] Although each point applies to both husband and wife, this table highlights some of the most influential factors in a marriage.

Five Things a Wife Loves in Her Husband	Five Things a Husband Loves in His Wife
A wife loves a husband who: 1. defends, protects and supports her; 2. patiently listens and converses with her; 3. expresses his affection for her through tender physical touches; 4. compliments her and shows interest in her; 5. makes her feel secure and safe in their relationship.	A husband loves a wife who: 1. respects his leadership, his role as a protector and provider; 2. makes an effort to look good for him and only him; 3. has confidence in his abilities and appreciates his efforts; 4. speaks well of him and his family; 5. keeps the marriage alive through physical touches.

---

56 Chapman, Gary D. 2010. *The Five Love Languages*. Farmington Hills, MI: Walker Large Print.
57 'The Book of Marital Secrets in the Light of the Book, *Sunnah* and Reality' by Dr. Jassim Al-Mutawa.

HOME SWEET HOME

A wife loves a husband who unhesitatingly defends, protects and supports her. She loves a husband who makes her feel as though she is his priority and who is attentive to her needs and wishes. She loves a husband who is a good listener and empathizes with her. In practice, this may mean he expresses appreciation for her sharing her thoughts, adding a few comments or even just remembering and mentioning a few bits later on to show he values her. A lot of stress is put on strengthening the emotional connection in marriages. This links to the second point which is that a wife loves a husband who touches her tenderly. These touches are gentle and not always sexual, e.g., a kiss on the forehead, a hug or other similar gentle touches. She also loves a husband who compliments her, shows interest in her and makes her feel secure and safe. A husband should never make his wife feel as though she is not enough for him or that he is no longer invested in their marriage.

Likewise, a husband loves certain things in his wife just as his wife loves certain things in her husband. More specifically, he loves a wife who respects him as a person and as a leader. The husband needs to have his leadership respected and his role as the provider and protector to be acknowledged. This is the extra degree of responsibility that Allah ﷻ has given him. It also means that when he falls short, he should not be ridiculed or belittled. Sometimes, when couples argue, they tend to

SPOUSES

claim that the other has never done anything for them or that they do not think the other has done enough. However, if either one of them really pondered on this statement, they would not be able to repeat it truthfully. Vocalizing such a lack of appreciation can adversely impact marital relationships and create a severe hostile environment at home. The other issue that may develop into a problem between couples relates to appearances. Both the husband and the wife should make an effort to look good for each other.

'Ikramah reported: Ibn Abbas, may Allah ﷻ be pleased with him, said, "Verily, I love to beautify myself for my wife, just as I love for her to beautify herself for me, due to the saying of Allah ﷻ Almighty: they have rights similar to those over them." [2: 228].[58]

The man's role as the protector and leader is brought into question if his wife only makes herself look good when she goes out but does not make any effort to do so when in the company of her husband. The same can be said of a husband who makes himself look immaculate when he is outside but never tries to do the same when he is at home. How a wife presents herself to her husband, or a husband to his wife is important. There is no need to abandon the kind of dress that makes the husband or wife comfortable and be forced to always

---

[58] al-Sunan al-Kubrá 14264

dress up. However, on occasion, it is important to try doing so for one's spouse. Both the husband and the wife should not allow the *Shayṭān* to meddle in their intimate relationship. They should also keep their marriage alive through physical touches. A husband loves a wife who initiates intimacy and affection between them and shows interest in this side of the marriage.

Acknowledging each other's efforts is also important for the maintenance of a healthy relationship between husband and wife. It means a lot for a spouse to hear, "I appreciate your efforts, I could not do it without you." Couples should not be stingy with their words of praise and appreciation; they should not allow their egos to stop them from giving positive verbal affirmations. The world is already replete with tests and trials, so it is important that the home is a place of solace, gratitude and happiness.

This means that husband and wife should always reflect the best versions of themselves. Publicly shaming and speaking poorly of one's spouse is detrimental, not only to one's relationship with their spouse, but also, to their relationship with other family members who may not forgive that easily if the marriage breaks up. The couple may find it easy to move on, but the families may hold on to their feelings of resentment for years. Moreover, involving other parties in matters concerning one's marriage, when there is no dire need for it, erases the boundaries of respect between spouses and increases the likelihood of unsolicited opinions which can quickly turn into much bigger problems.

At the onset of any conflict between the spouses, it may seem easy to use the home as a place to vent out one's anger and disappointment. However, continuously complaining about stress coming from outside of the home can elevate the tension levels in the home. Some distance should therefore be created between life in the home and life outside the home for the betterment of the couple's inner peace and marriage.

Unattractive Traits

Traits a Husband Finds Unattractive in a Wife	Traits a Wife Finds Unattractive in a Husband
1. Possessing masculine traits at the expense of her femininity;	1. Possessing feminine traits at the expense of his masculinity;
2. Verbally aggressive by constantly shouting loudly;	2. Not possessing the ability to make decisions independently or confidently;
3. Taking charge of his duties;	3. Inconsistency, unreliability and constant lying;
4. Carelessness and over-demanding of his money that he spends on her;	4. Stinginess;
5. Neglecting herself physically.	5. Being insecure and emotionally immature.

*Although, one may argue that the above traits can apply to each spouse equally, I have listed them based on what is predominant in most husbands and wives.

HOME SWEET HOME

A husband finds it unattractive when his wife is constantly overwhelmed by negative emotions, such as anger, especially if this manifests into verbal aggression and amplifies her personal attacks on him. It is a form of ingratitude to highlight and enumerate her husband's faults and ignore all the good traits he possesses. Using her voice to abuse her husband is psychologically damaging to him as well as to others. A factor that contributes to this is having a loud voice that dominates conversations and inhibits other opinions. This strips the wife of her softness and femininity which is attractive to her husband. In the same way, a husband should be capable of managing and controlling his emotions.

Husbands also find it unattractive when their wives insinuate that they think they are incompetent. Most often this happens in the course of child-rearing. A husband may be changing his child's nappy, and the wife may jump in and take over, or he is prevented from making choices for his family and often excluded from decision-making. Even if the wife changes nappies better, suggesting that her husband is inept in looking after his child, or repeatedly comparing him to other men or fathers, can be harmful to their marriage.

As common as it may be, it is insulting to a man to say that he is babysitting his own child or he is on 'daddy duty' when he is simply being a parent. The suggestion that he is a peripheral figure in the family rather than a pivotal figure harms the marriage and the family dynamic.

In a similar vein, a wife finds it unattractive if her husband has a weak personality and lacks confidence. If a man is unable to make his own decisions and relies on his parents or siblings to make them for him, he inadvertently demonstrates his incompetence as a leader. Of course, asking advice from others is important and valuable, but what is criticized and disliked here is the man who has no independent thoughts or opinions. Rather, a man should include his wife in decision-making about the family so that important discussions take place, and concerns are raised and voiced. Both the husband and the wife should consult one another regarding appointments or family activities and should not exclude each other from matters that concern them both.

Unreliability, inconsistency and dishonesty are other traits that women hate and can cause a wife to lose respect for her husband. When a man is stingy and does not like to spend on his family, this creates a strain on his marriage and harms his image in his wife's eyes. Furthermore, it is a sign of emotional immaturity and insecurity in a man when he degrades his wife to feel good and elevated. Such a behaviour imprints in the mind of the wife an image and opinion of her husband which can be difficult to erase.

Both husband and wife should make conscientious decisions and always consider how to improve their relationship.

Rights and Duties in a Marriage

There is a narration, which scholars of *ḥadīth* have disputed regarding its reliability, with some saying that it has a 'weak chain of narration and issues with some of its wordings' and others say it is 'acceptable'. In summary, the general message is that a woman has a right to refuse a marriage proposal. The narration says that a woman during the time of the Prophet ﷺ refused to get married. She was adamant and could not be persuaded. Her father complained to the Prophet ﷺ saying, "O Messenger of Allah ﷺ, my daughter is growing old and she is refusing to marry. What should I do?" The Prophet ﷺ asked the father if he could speak to the daughter and when he questioned her, she said, "O Messenger of Allah ﷺ, I refuse to get married until I know what Allah ﷻ is going to ask me about my duties towards the man I marry. What do I have to do? I need to know what his rights are."

This woman was not even concerned about her own rights. She was concerned with the man's rights. Rightly so, she had recognized that marriage is an act of worship

SPOUSES

and feared Allah ﷻ regarding it. She knew that Allah ﷻ would question her on whether or not she discharged the rights of her husband.

So, the Prophet ﷺ told her about the rights of both husband and wife in a marriage. Upon learning them, she found herself still not ready and said, "O Messenger of Allah ﷺ, I am not ready to fulfil that yet. I need to go back and think about it." So, he said to her father,

"You can not force her. Leave her until she is ready."[59]

It is one's Islamic duty to know their rights and the rights of others, so that they are not exploited or taken advantage of, or that they do not exploit or take advantage of others.

A woman once came to the Prophet ﷺ and said, "O Messenger of Allah, my father forced me to marry this particular man and I did not want to, but I had no choice."

The Prophet ﷺ said to her, "It is up to you: you can either remain married to him or, if you want, I can divorce you from him."

She replied, "I will accept my father's decision and stay with him."[60]

---

[59] Ibn Abu Shaybah in his "Musannaf" (3/556), an-Nasa'i in "Sunna al-Kubra' (3/283), al-Bazzar in "Kash al-Astar" (1465) and al-Baihaqy in his "Sunan al-Kubra" (7/291). Reliability of *ḥadīth*: disputed between weak and acceptable

[60] Reported by an-Nas'i (3217) and similar in Ibn Majah (1874). See also: https://islamqa.info/amp/en/answers/4602

Her marriage was first presented as an arranged marriage and then came to fit the definition of a forced marriage. She had been coerced and forced into a marriage she did not want. The Prophet ﷺ did not force her into a decision but instead presented her with two options. In the end, she decided for herself – a right she had all along but one she was not aware of. We must teach women (and men) about their rights so that they can make decisions for themselves. This was a reflection made by the woman herself and she was pleased to know her rights, because she said, "I wanted the other women to know that, in Islam, women have the right to refuse being forced to marry or that their father marry them off without their consent."[61]

It is important, on a societal level, to teach these rights early on so that women and men are not coerced into accepting decisions made on their behalf. Often, family members may make these huge decisions for a person and this is why setting clear boundaries early on can be beneficial.

People can be consumed with dictating the lives of their children – which is normal when they are very young – but it should not be to such an extent that they forget

---

[61] Reported by an-Nas'i (3217) and similar in Ibn Majah (1874). Judgement of review based on Sahih Muslim's criteria of sahih ḥadīths. See also: https://islamqa.info/amp/ar/answers/163990

that they have their own minds and can use their own judgements. They tend to clip their children's wings and find excuses for doing so because they believe that they have already experienced the world and therefore know infinitely more than their children will ever know.

Arranged – not forced – marriages are allowed in Islam, but they are not the only option. An arranged marriage is a lawful option which involves the families of two prospective spouses. However, sometimes children can also find, or recommend, a prospective spouse for themselves, and they should not be deprived of such an option. Arranged marriages are called so because a choice is arranged between two parties and both have the right to accept or reject this offered choice. Compulsion, pressure and emotional blackmail per definition disqualifies it from being an arranged marriage. Parents are obliged to accept their children's decision if they reject a proposal for marriage, or even change their mind about it at a later stage. Parents can advise and guide, but when it comes to the final decision, they must step back and allow their children to make their own decisions.

In some cases, parents force their children to divorce their spouses due to, perhaps, an internal conflict within the marriage which the couple themselves have moved on from. Problems sometimes arise because other family members are unable to accept a spouse or get along with him or her. This is a form of oppression, and it is unlawful. It is a sin to force one's daughter or son to divorce their spouse without a justified legal reason.

The *Sharīʿah* clearly defines the rights of marriage. Relationships should not, however, revolve only around rights and duties. These rights and duties should not be regular topics of discussion, thrown around casually in the household or used as threats. Relationships should be based on love, respect, understanding, peace, tranquillity, mercy, sincerity, goodness, giving more than ought to be given, and going beyond what is obligated in the hope of bringing each other closer. When all these elements are present in a marriage, everyone automatically gets their rights. One may sometimes feel that their rights are violated. If this is the case, they need to address this issue with their spouse in a compassionate and kind manner. Doing so will increase love between them. When there is a conflict between the spouses and there is no obvious solution at hand, a mediator or judge may be recommended for the couple to evaluate mutual rights in their relationship. Rights and obligations are given so that one has a yardstick through which they can navigate. Relationships between spouses should extend far beyond rights and duties, even if these are the foundation on which a marriage is built. In times of conflict, these rights and duties can be consulted to put to rest any major issues.

SPOUSES

One should claim their rights without guilt so that they are able to maintain boundaries. For example, if a son is grappling with a delicate issue between his wife and mother, he can turn to the *Sharī'ah* for guidance and refer to it as a form of evidenced-based support. The *Sharī'ah* clearly sets out what is right and what is wrong, which can put an end to any conflict without going round in circles. Our morals and standards should be based on the laws Allah ﷻ has sent down for us.

Allah ﷻ says in the Qur'ān,

$$وَمِنْ ءَايَـٰتِهِ أَنْ خَلَقَ لَكُم مِّنْ أَنفُسِكُمْ أَزْوَٰجًا لِّتَسْكُنُوٓا إِلَيْهَا وَجَعَلَ بَيْنَكُم مَّوَدَّةً وَرَحْمَةً إِنَّ فِى ذَٰلِكَ لَءَايَـٰتٍ لِّقَوْمٍ يَتَفَكَّرُونَ$$

And of His Signs is that He has created mates for you from your own kind that you may find peace in them and He has set between you love and mercy. Surely there are signs in this for those who reflect.[62]

Marriage is not a contract set in stone, requiring no flexibility whatsoever. The relationship between spouses should not mirror the relationship one has with a business partner or a colleague. It should not be based on just rights and responsibilities. It should not be a formal relationship akin to a business transaction with no feelings or deep emotions involved therein. Allah ﷻ speaks of marriage using words such as compassion, mercy and kindness.

---

62 Surah al-Rūm 30: 21

HOME SWEET HOME

Marriage brings together different lives and personalities and spouses should have between them a degree of flexibility and understanding rooted in their love for one another. Essentially, a certain space for error must be allowed as perfection should never be expected. Every single person has a different way of processing emotions, personalities and beliefs. As products of their own environment, people are shaped by their experiences and by their genetics, biochemistry and brain structure. It is therefore imperative not to second-guess another person's intention. One should sit down and communicate their thoughts and make an effort to listen to their spouse. It could be the case that they must communicate how to manage and deal with certain family members. In any case, spouses should ensure that they are on the same page so that a concerted effort is made to avoid, or at least minimize, further conflicts.

Allah ﷻ says in the Qur'ān,

وَعَاشِرُوهُنَّ بِالْمَعْرُوفِ

Live with them [your wives] gracefully.[63]

What does it mean to live with wives 'gracefully'?

Living gracefully with them means one should live with them in a kind and fair manner. The first manifestation

---

63   Surah al-Nisā' 4: 19

of this is that one lives with them in goodness and not harm them physically, verbally, mentally or emotionally. The second is that they should actively demonstrate acts of kindness to one another. Lastly, they should not delay or neglect their obligations towards each other.

The rights of spouses towards each other are a blessing on them and the *Sharīʿah* has outlined them so that they are aware of their duties towards each other. The *Sharīʿah* is the criterion through which one ascertains whether their actions are sinful. It settles disputes when there is a need for intervention and draws a line between a person's right and what is considered a form of oppression. Knowing one's rights and the rights of others establishes clear boundaries and makes one aware of where they stand and where others do.

It is important for a man, the leader of the household, to know how to differentiate between his rights and the rights of his wife and mother. Often, the man is pulled in different directions due to societal and family pressures, which has an adverse effect on his relationship with those closest to him. If his wife sees him succumbing to the wishes of his mother at the expense of her rights, she loses respect for him and questions his manhood. She may feel abandoned, isolated and dismissed and therefore think that she deserves a man who does not bend to the will of others and can make his own decisions confidently – using the *Sharīʿah* as his guide. She may think that she deserves better than a man who is externally controlled by others in decisions regarding his family and household. Likewise, a wife should not let her side of the family dictate her relationship with her husband, children and household.

Nonetheless, the *Sharīʿah* is the voice of reason and has the power to resolve such issues. If the husband and wife do their duties as Allah ﷻ has commanded, their mutual rights will be automatically maintained. The rights and duties outlined by the *Sharīʿah* are the bare minimum and relationships are much more complex and should be much deeper than the confines of rights and duties.

It is through generosity that love grows, and one should be most generous in the love they give.

Allah ﷻ has allocated rights according to His wisdom and one must accept them even though they are not the same for men and women. Going against Allah's commandments will inevitably lead to negative repercussions. Allah ﷻ has taken into account the different natures of men and women, which is why Islamic guidelines are informed by the notions of femininity and masculinity. The rights of the husband and those of the wife may be said to be counterbalanced. If a husband has a certain right over his wife, his wife has a counter

"Women have the same rights against their men as men have against them; but men have a degree above them. Allah is All-powerful, All-wise."

right over him. These rights are allotted by Allah ﷻ in a fair and appropriate manner which ensures a harmonious family, healthy enough to raise children well and in their best interests. Both husband and wife may at times fall short of their rights and duties, and this is where patience and communication are imperative.

Regarding the rights and duties of the husband and wife, there is only one right in which the husband has one degree of extra responsibility over his wife. The Qur'ān uses the term *Qiwamah* for this which means 'leadership'. It is the right of the husband to lead his wife, direct her, spend on her and protect her. Therefore, he should make decisions in her best interests and treat her well. Often, in times of conflict, the wife can and should use this right to her own advantage and remind her husband that it is her right to be led, protected and maintained. A woman's exclusive ability to bear children, give birth and breastfeed her children necessitates that she has support and guidance from her husband. At first glance, it may seem that the husband is in a superior position because of this, but it is clear from Qur'ānic verses that Allah ﷻ sees men and women as equal. A wife can be superior to her husband in the eyes of Allah ﷻ because Allah ﷻ judges people according to their intentions, the state of their hearts and the conditions in which they are placed.

In *Sūrah al-Taḥrīm*, Allah ﷻ gives the example of the wife of Pharaoh, Āsiyah ؓ, may Allah ﷻ be pleased with her, who followed the Prophet Mūsā's ﷺ message and believed in one God, despite her husband's vehement opposition to Mūsā ﷺ. His enmity towards Islam and Allah ﷻ destined him for hell. In contrast, Āsiyah's righteousness was so noteworthy that she was included among the four women whose faith was perfected. Her superiority to Pharaoh was not because of her wealth or status, but rather due to the strength of her faith.

Islam does not condone that the husband behaves as a dictator. Allah ﷻ did not say the husband is the boss or that he owns his family. He commanded the husband to live with his wife in goodness and fairness, demonstrating that Islam does not permit abusing that right and turning it into a form of control and coercion. Abusing and manipulating these rights and duties is unlawful. A man may not be able to show his compassion or may not possess the emotional intelligence required in a marriage to start with. These skills need to be learned and honed. If they are not learned and applied, the breakdown of the family begins slowly until it collapses and then questions are raised about how the breakdown began in the first place.

Islam also teaches that a wife should help her husband

and motivate him. She should make him feel confident enough to be a leader, maintainer and protector. Relationships can break down because the husband perceives that his wife seeks to emasculate him and change his true identity. This can lead to the husband not having the opportunity to exercise his rights and increases family tension.

Allah ﷻ says in the Qur'ān,

$$وَلَهُنَّ مِثْلُ الَّذِي عَلَيْهِنَّ بِالْمَعْرُوفِ ۚ وَلِلرِّجَالِ عَلَيْهِنَّ دَرَجَةٌ ۗ وَاللَّهُ عَزِيزٌ حَكِيمٌ$$

Women have the same rights against their men as men have against them; but men have a degree above them. Allah is All-powerful, All-wise.[64]

Let us observe here how Allah ﷻ describes Himself as the One who has power and not the husband. This is because the husband is expected to follow the commands of Allah ﷻ. The above verse is a reminder to the husband that his responsibility is not about showcasing his superiority towards his wife but to fulfil his duty towards Allah ﷻ first and foremost. Accepting the implications of these names of Allah ﷻ should be enough to reassure both husband and wife that this is in their best interests. They must hold themselves accountable and accept that Allah ﷻ will surely hold them accountable

---

64   Surah al-Baqarah 2: 228

too. He is the One who has power and He is the One who should be feared most.

Mutual rights

1. Treating each other well

2. Creating a safe space

3. Maintaining family ties

Both husband and wife should strive to please each other. They should excel in their treatment and continually reflect on how they can improve to be a better life companion. If physical, verbal, emotional, mental or sexual needs are unmet, then they need to be prioritized in the marriage and discussed at length.

The Prophet ﷺ instructed husbands to be tender and gentle with their wives and wives to be appreciative of their husbands' efforts. He ﷺ used to share food with his wives. 'Ā'ishah related, "I used to eat the meat from a bone when I was menstruating, then the Messenger of Allah ﷺ would take it and put his mouth where my mouth had been. And I would drink from a vessel, and the Messenger of Allah ﷺ would take it and put his mouth where my mouth had been, and I was menstruating."[65] Through this, he showed his love and

---

65 Sunan Ibn Majah, ḥadīth 643, Chapter: 3, The Chapters on Dry Ablution

affection for her. Even when she was menstruating, he was physically intimate with her in different ways and made an effort to dispel any doubts about her purity. He used to race with her and be playful with her, never allowing his role as The Last Messenger to deprive his family of his love.

The love between the Prophet ﷺ and his family was palpable and exhaustively documented in *ḥadīth* literature. Anas ؓ narrated, the Prophet ﷺ was with one of his wives, when one of the Mothers of the Believers sent a bowl in which there was some food. The one in whose house the Prophet ﷺ was, struck the hand of the servant, and the bowl fell and broke. The Prophet ﷺ picked up the pieces of the bowl. Then he began to collect the food that was in it, and said, "Your mother got jealous." Then he exchanged the broken bowl with an unbroken one from the house he was staying and gave it to the servant. He gave the intact bowl to the one whose bowl had been broken, and he kept the broken bowl in the house of the one who had broken it.[66] Here, he showed understanding for her feelings and demonstrated his sense of fairness by sending one of her plates filled with food to the other wife, as compensation. He did acknowledge that what she did was not right, but he dealt with the situation wisely. This demonstration of

---

66 Sahih al-Bukhari (5225)

compassion and understanding can be easily applied to many marital contexts.

Another right of marriage is that the husband and wife must safeguard each other's dignity and honour. They should respect each other's personal property, which means they should not check on each other's personal devices without permission. Transparency in terms of who one spends their time with and where is important, and here communication is needed. Spouses should not be elusive about their whereabouts or who they are seeing because this may lead to suspicion and the other spouse may use deceitful means to find out about the matter, which is unlawful.

Allah ﷻ says,

$$\text{يَا أَيُّهَا الَّذِينَ آمَنُوا اجْتَنِبُوا كَثِيرًا مِّنَ الظَّنِّ}$$

Believers, avoid being excessively suspicious...[67]

Using deceitful means, after exhausting all other means, to find out where one's spouse is and with whom, may be excusable if they have good reasons to believe that the harmony of their family is under threat. However, it is more appropriate to use other means such as discussing the issue. Even when there is suspicion that a spouse has committed a form of betrayal, or there is some

---

67 Surah al-Ḥujurāt 49: 12

perceived harm, such a suspicion should not be based on paranoia but on well-founded facts. Spying because of paranoia or over protectiveness is unlawful. The best way of dealing with a scenario such as this lies in talking, communication and discussion with one's spouse. One should be honest about their concerns and suspicions and then see how they can work through this together with their spouse.

Another right of marriage is that both the husband and wife must respect each other's family and develop a good relationship with them. Both should maintain these family ties and help each other to maintain them. Some husbands assert coercive control over their wives and use religion to prevent their wives from leaving their homes and seeing their families. Islam does not give a husband the right to order his wife to cut off her family ties unless there is direct harm coming from that relationship. A wife has the right to disobey her husband if he prevents her from seeing her family. The same goes for the wife: she cannot stop her husband from seeing his family or force him to cut off his family ties. It is important to remember that marriage does not mean that a spouse no longer has any duties towards his extended family.

The Prophet ﷺ honoured the friends of his late wife

Khadījah ﷺ. Once 'Ā'ishah ﷺ saw the Prophet ﷺ talking and laughing with an elderly woman. She asked him,

مَن تِلْكَ العَجُوزِ يَا رَسُولَ اللهِ؟

"Who is that old woman, O Messenger of Allah?"

He said, "She is a friend of Khadījah; we were just remembering the good old days."[68]

'Ā'ishah ﷺ said,

قد أبدَلَكَ اللهُ عزَّ وجلَّ بها خَيرًا منها

"Allah most High and exalted has replaced you with a better one than her [meaning herself]"[69]

The Prophet ﷺ said,

"By Allah ﷻ, no! She supported me when everyone else deserted me; she believed me when everyone else called me a liar; she gave me her home when I was homeless; and Allah ﷻ gave me children from her."[70]

ما أبدَلَني اللهُ عزَّ وجلَّ خَيرًا منها.

"No, He did not give me a better wife."

---

68 As-Silsilah as-Sahihah (the authentic list of *hadīths*), al-Albani, 1/424. And in al-Hakim in 'al-Mustadrak', ch 1, page 166 (Arabic version)
69 Bukhari (3821), Muslim (2437) and Ahmad (24864)
70 Bukhari (3821), Muslim (2437) and Ahmad (24864)

'Ā'ishah ؓ stated that she was never more jealous of any woman than she was of Khadījah ؓ, even though she had passed away. And from that day, she said, "I never said a single word about Khadījah ؓ."[71]

One of the lessons we take from this is that we should always honour those connected to our spouse. By doing so, we strengthen the marital bond and follow in the footsteps of the Prophet ﷺ.

Rights of a Wife

1. The *mahr*, dowry, upon marriage
2. Day-to-day living expenditure
3. Independent housing

The *mahr* is the first right of a wife and should be agreed upon before the marriage contract (*nikāḥ*) is concluded. It is the wife's right to obtain her *mahr* before the marriage is consummated, but it can be paid at a later date if she agrees.

Allah ﷻ says about the *mahr* in *Sūrah Nisā'*,

وَءَاتُوا ٱلنِّسَآءَ صَدُقَٰتِهِنَّ نِحْلَةً ۚ فَإِن طِبْنَ لَكُمْ عَن شَىْءٍ مِّنْهُ

---

71 Bukhari 6004, Book 78, *ḥadīth* 35. Also see Vol. 8, Book 73, *ḥadīth* 33

SPOUSES

$$\text{نَفْسًا فَكُلُوهُ هَنِيئًا مَّرِيئًا}$$

Give women their bridal due in good cheer (considering it a duty); but if they willingly remit any part of it, consume it with good pleasure [72]

The *mahr* is a symbol of honesty and goodwill; a promise from the husband that he will honour her rights and care for her. It is symbolic of her right to own her own property and independence from her husband. She has the right to ask for what she wants, which could be jewellery, tuition fees or even a *Ḥajj* trip. Some cultures have their own norms, and if a woman wishes to follow them, she can do so. For example, in Lebanon, it is common to give thousands of dollars' worth of jewellery and furniture as a *mahr*. It is not an Islamic practice to exaggerate the value of *mahr* but as a cultural norm it is acceptable if it is affordable.

The Prophet ﷺ said regarding the *mahr*,

"Facilitate matters; do not make marriage difficult."

Nowadays, the value of *mahr* is extremely extortionate and used for boasting and pride. Therefore, it is important not to overlook the above directive of the Prophet ﷺ.

---

[72] Surah al-Nisā' 4: 4

Another right that a wife has over her husband is that he should pay for her day-to-day living expenses. This includes food, drink, clothing, medical expenses, transport for her needs, hygiene products, and some jurists even say beauty products, provided that they are used appropriately.[73] If it is in his means, he should spend on her more than this and be generous so that the love between them increases.

In *Sūrah Baqarah*, Allah ﷻ, says,

$$وَعَلَى الْمَوْلُودِ لَهُ رِزْقُهُنَّ وَكِسْوَتُهُنَّ بِالْمَعْرُوفِ$$

[In such a case] it is incumbent upon him who has begotten the child to provide them (i.e. divorced women) their sustenance and clothing in a fair manner...[74]

The Prophet ﷺ said, "Men must provide for them, clothe them and give them *bi-l-maʿrūf*."[75] *Bi-l-maʿrūf* means that she is treated like other women of her standing or 'in a fitting manner', in accordance with the standards of her community. It is also the woman's right to work and provide for herself if she wishes to do so and there are

---

73 The Maliki jurists in 'Ash-Sharh as-Sagheer' by ad-Dardeer al-Maliki; The Shafi'i jurists in 'Al-Haawi' by Mawardi ash-shafi'i (Both in Arabic). Here are a couple of reference from islamweb:
https://www.islamweb.net/amp/en/fatwa/461959/
https://www.islamweb.net/amp/ar/fatwa/344974/
74 Surah al-Baqarah 2: 233
75 Muslim, 1218

no valid objections by her husband. Some valid objections may be that the work environment or nature of the work is forbidden in Islam. It may also be that it diverts too much time and attention away from the family in a way that results in her abandoning her duties to her family. Work does not necessarily mean outside of the home, as she can work from home or invest in permissible shares. Invalid objections vary. However, if it was agreed upon before the marriage contract that the wife can work, then the husband is not permitted to forbid her afterwards without her approval. This is because of the Prophet's teaching, 'Muslims must stick to their agreements and conditions'.[76]

The Qur'ān also teaches men to be generous with their wives: to give them beyond what has been obligated, and to live with them on good terms. If they have to divorce them, it should be done amicably. Allah speaks about the love between the husband and wife using the term *mawaddah* which means deep love. Families may also suffer some financial difficulties, a matter which is documented in *ḥadīth* literature. After accepting Islam, Hind, the wife of Abū Sufyān went once to see the Prophet and said, "O Messenger of Allah, Abū Sufyān is very stingy; he does not give me what is

---

76 Sahih Abu Dawud, 3594 and Ibn Habban 5091

enough for me and my children. So, can I take from his money without his knowledge?"

He said to her,

"Yes, you can do so."[77]

Through this, we can see that a wife has the right to take from her husband what is due to her. This is limited, however, to what she needs and not what she wants, and hence she should not exploit her husband. The husband's financial situation should be taken into account, and the wife has to be considerate. If the husband is the one who is managing the money, saving up, and looking after his wife's affairs, then calling him stingy is unfair. The Prophet ﷺ said,

"The best spending is what one spends on one's family."[78]

The husband has no right to his wife's personal wealth without her permission; nor does he have any right to tell her where she should spend or even donate it. This is established in the following *ḥadīth*:

Umāmah ؓ said, "O Messenger of Allah ﷺ, I donated my wealth to so-and-so."

And he said to her, "Had you donated it to your uncles

---

77 Sahih al-Bukhari, Vol. 7, Book 64, no. 272
78 Sahih Muslim 995, Book 12, *ḥadīth* 48. Also see Book 5, *ḥadīth* 2181.

and aunts, you would have gotten more reward: the reward of kinship and the reward of donation."[79]

Here, he did not command or order her but he reminded her that she can donate without his permission and offered her good advice. A husband has no right to question his wife about her own financial dealings nor take control over her money.

It is important to discuss financial matters because more often than not, they are the root cause of conflict at home. In Islam, financial autonomy is given to both husband and wife, and both are encouraged to help one another so that love between them increases. Managing money is a daily occurrence in any household. If a wife decides to help her husband financially, then this is considered a charity from her part towards her husband. There is no obligation on her to provide financial assistance nor is there any restriction on this. Both husband and wife may even have separate bank accounts, and a wife may even lend her husband money to settle financial issues relating to their home.

Spouses should set clear boundaries and expectations regarding finances in their household, just as they should make an effort to learn their rights.

---

[79] Sahih al-Bukhari 2592 and Muslim 999

HOME SWEET HOME

A wife also has a right to her own independent home with all of its amenities. In some cultures, it is the norm to live with one's in-laws, but this is the dictate of culture and not of Islam. Parents may even command their son and his wife to live with them, but this means depriving the wife of her right.

In some cases, a wife may agree to live with her in-laws, and, in this case, it is a charity from her that Allah ﷻ will reward her for. Scholars, however, advise that one should not live with their parents once married unless there is a dire need. This is the majority opinion among the jurists of the Hanafi, Shafi'i and Hanbali schools.[80] This is because conflicts within the home can escalate and destroy multiple relationships at the same time. Keeping a certain distance is important and this means that one should not even live too close to each other. Independence needs to be gained, and the couple should be able to live their lives together without interference from other family members. The experts say, "Do not cut them off completely but do not be clingy."[81]

---

80 https://islamqa.info/amp/en/answers/7653; https://fiqh.islamonline.net/en/dealing-with-in-laws-from-an-islamic-viewpoint/; https://fiqh.islamonline.net/كيفية-التوفيق-بين-حقوق-الزوجة،-
text=~:#/وحقوق-ا فالجمع بين الأبوين والزوجة في,الفقهاء من الحنفية والشافعية
والحنابلة.١

81 Dr. Jasem Al-Matawa, in his podcast at the following link:
https://wwwyoutube.com/watch?v=oZ3BRvPdFrc
[Accessed 25 Aug. 2024]

SPOUSES

They stress that a balance is needed between navigating one's relationship with their spouse and their parents. Maintaining a healthy relationship is of paramount importance and so decisions need to be made with this aim in mind.

It is easy to feel angry and bitter in the process of divorce, and one may be tempted to believe that they deserve a return on their goodness. This is why Allah ﷻ in the Qur'ān stresses an amicable separation between the spouses.

Rights of a husband

1. To be respected as the leader of the household
2. Protect his family
3. Intimacy
4. To have his wealth and property guarded
5. His wife must guard her chastity

Allah ﷻ has given the man the responsibility of leading his family in making better decisions together and live their lives in accordance to Allah's laws. This responsibility means that he is accountable for the state of the family whose harmony he must ensure.

Allah ﷻ said, "A creature is not to be obeyed when it involves disobedience to the Creator."[82]

Therefore, a husband cannot command his wife to do anything sinful, and he must uphold the standards of good conduct and morals and encourage them in his household.

Allah ﷻ says,

$$وَتَعَاوَنُوا عَلَى البِرِّ وَالتَّقوٰى$$

Help one another in acts of righteousness and piety [83]

This means that husbands should help in raising the spiritual well-being of their spouses, as well as help them in any other ways.

Many studies have shown that men have more frequent and intense sexual desires than women. Therefore, the right to an intimate relationship is more stressed for a husband. Both husband and wife must show tenderness towards each other through intimacy. Ḥadīth literature showcases the needs of both husband and wife.

Another right of a husband over his wife is that she protects his wealth and property. This means the wife is responsible for not inviting harm on her husband,

---

82 Mishkat al-Masabih 3696, Book 18, ḥadīth 36 & Ahmad 1041
83 Surah al-Maidah 5: 2

his wealth or his property. He also has a right over his wife that she guards her chastity in his absence. This means that she differentiates herself as a married woman and does not have contact with non-*mahram* men when she is alone.

It is the right of a husband to undertake safety and preventative measures to protect his family. This may mean that certain individuals are not allowed in his house, and his wife must uphold this.

In-Laws

Can boundaries be set respectfully?

How can couples remain united when issues with the in-laws arise?

Boundary Setting

When two families unite through marriage, a bond is sealed between them and this bond needs to be maintained and protected. Even if a couple gets divorced, their father-in-law and mother-in-law remain *maḥrams* forever. Moreover, grandchildren have the right to keep in touch with their grandparents, even in the event of divorce. In-laws therefore have a right to courtesy and respect.

Imagine a big circle with two circles inside it, one medium and one small. The first inner circle represents the husband and wife. This circle covers the discussion of private affairs. These should be kept confidential and

Establishing the 3 privacy circles

What should we share with whom?

- Friends / public
- Family
- Husband & Wife

never leave this circle. If a husband and wife want to increase love between them and minimize problems, then things between them should not be shared with anyone else, especially not on social media.

The second circle encompasses the spouses' families, parents and siblings. The private matters of all those who are in this circle must remain within this circle and not be divulged to anyone outside of it.

The third circle, the largest circle, is the one that is shared with the public.

In the modern world, these lines are blurred, which explains why divorce rates, marital conflicts and toxic marriages are on the rise. Nowadays, private matters are filled with countless outside opinions. The fault of this often lies with the couple themselves who have allowed the interference. Another factor impacting divorce rates is excessive individualism. This means people's primary concern is themselves and they are not prepared to put others first, forgive or overlook other people's mistakes and shortcomings.

As far as marital privacy is concerned, clear boundaries must be set from the onset, and other people who attempt to pry must be told to stop. Spouses should not invite them into thinking that they are doing them or themselves a favour, as this will backfire against them. Spouses can still behave kindly towards others without divulging to them details about their family life.

Sharing details of marital disagreements and disputes with other people can lead to disastrous consequences. Spouses are bound to have occasional conflicts and disagreements due to their closeness and intimate relationship. In the beginning of their marriage, they might be still closer to members of their family than they are to each other. Hence, when one of them slips or makes a mistake, the other spouse may reach out to other family members about it rather than learn how to deal with the situation and adapt. Even if a conflict is resolved within a few hours and one spouse forgives the other, the spouses are not privy to each other's thoughts and feelings and resentment may still linger between them, which adversely affects their marriage.

In general, fathers-in-law and mothers-in-law tend to think that their own children are faultless. When their children have a conflict or dispute with their spouses, they may hold a grudge against them that lasts for years. They may form an opinion that the spouse is a bad person and undeserving of their son or daughter. For this reason, spouses should not talk to their parents about everything that happens in their marital home; nor should they follow everything their parents tell them. As parents, they deserve more respect than other family members or people, but this does not mean they have the right to dictate how their married children live their lives. Such a boundary does not need to be set in a hostile manner; it could be set even by just acknowledging their opinions and thoughts, kissing them on the forehead and respectfully asking them to step back, so that the matter is dealt with privately.

It is also advisable for spouses to live separately from their in-laws. Privacy in a marriage is important and Allah ﷻ will question one about the rights they owe others. Living separately and away from in-laws will reduce stress and make it easier to uphold the rights of one's spouse.

Another right is the right of the mother and father to name and raise their children. In some cultures, the parents of the husband think they have the right to oblige him to name his children after them. If their wishes are not met, marital strain may ensue which can lead to divorce, or severed family ties, which is a major sin. Islamically speaking, the husband and wife have the right to name their children and no conflict should arise because of this issue. The husband's parents should be reminded that love is not shown by naming their grandchildren after them. Rather, love is shown through one's treatment. After all, the Prophet ﷺ did not name his children after those in his lineage nor did the companions.

Sometimes conflict arises because of competing demands: the demands of one's parents and those of their spouse. When this occurs, it seems as though one is in an impossible situation. What one can do in such situations is to obey their parents when their demand involves only themselves, such as taking their mother to an appointment or helping their father with some chores. If the demand also involves one's wife, then they do not have to acquiesce to the demands of their parents. For example, some parents pressurize their children to have a baby and set time limits for them. They may even state their preferred gender. The husband and wife alone have the right to make decisions regarding having children and, if it is Allah's will to deny a wife to be pregnant or delay her pregnancy, the family should respect Allah's will without blaming the husband and wife.

A couple I know in Lebanon lived in the same building as the husband's parents. The parents lived in an apartment above the couple's apartment, and every time the son returned home, he would go to his wife first. His mother would notice that he came to her after seeing his wife and became jealous. The wife discussed this issue with her husband and advised him to see his mother first. She told him to go first to his mother, laugh and joke with her, tell her how much he loved her and then come to her. Although there was nothing wrong with seeing his wife first, the wife sought to maintain harmony in the family. Due to other family members' immaturity or personalities, one may be forced to bend to their wishes to accommodate them. One must adapt their approach and behaviour towards other family members so that their connection with them is not lost and so rights are maintained.

Likewise, when the family gets together for a positive activity, those married into the family are under no obligation to join in. For example, some family members may decide to set a donation box for a good cause. The siblings may have agreed to take part, but the spouses who have married into the family do not necessarily have to follow suit and no one has the right to question their judgement or label them negatively because of it.

Some customs and traditions dictate that a wife must

help in the house of her in-laws, just as a daughter would. If the wife does help out of her own goodwill, then it will help foster love and strengthen the relationship. However, she is not obliged to do so. There should not be an expectation that she must cater to the entire household or even have responsibilities assigned to her.

In order to foster love, it is necessary to make an effort to create harmony, which means that one must go beyond and above their rights and duties. One should strive to ensure that they have a good relationship with their in-laws, even if they have to go an extra mile. They should always strive to be good to their in-laws and deal with any arising issues with them quickly and efficiently.

If there is a conflict between the husband and wife, they must work together as a team and address any issues head on. They must come to mutual agreements together.

"In order to foster love, it is necessary to make an effort to create harmony, which means that one must go beyond and above their rights and duties."

Conclusion

This book is by no means an exhaustive guide on how to create harmony in one's home. It serves only as a general guide through which better understanding may be gained of people's rights and duties in terms of family relationships. It is hoped that divorced couples, single-parent families, reconstituted families, and even those who are not married or do not have children can also benefit from this book.

In my counselling career, I have often noticed a pattern in family discords. When family members presented their grievances, their complaints were a list of violations of their own rights and lack of the other person's duties and responsibilities. While rights, duties and boundaries are comprehensively detailed in Islamic *Sharī'ah*, through taking a holistic view of the Islamic teachings one can realize and strongly sense that it focuses the attention in relationships on love, kindness and mercy, and less on

CONCLUSION

rights and duties. The rights and duties are only set out as a standard guideline to fall back on during times of conflict, as a basis for legal resolution, rulings and fairness.

However, since human beings are a creation with complex emotions and sensitivities, a healthy relationship filled with harmony, love and understanding can only be reached by being mutually 'flexible' with one's own rights, lowering the degree of expectations between each other and doing more than just the minimum duties set out in Islam. The Quran and prophetic examples constantly direct the attention of family members to show gratitude and appreciation of each other's goodness, services and virtues and focus less on one's own virtues. The key words in the Quran around which all family treatment should nurture are *sakeenah*- tranquillity and peace, and *mawaddah* and *rahmah*. *Mawaddah* is an Arabic word to which I could not find an English equivalence. In general, it means the genuine and thoughtful acts of kindness and services one gives of their own accord to another person to attract their hearts but are not coupled with constant reminders of their own good they have done. It is considered the 'source of love', which nurtures the growth of love between the spouses and family members.

However, for it to be successful, it must be mutual. The third key word is *rahmah*, which means mercy. This is of paramount importance in the family since humans are always prone to mistakes and shortcomings. Mercy diminishes conflicts, and promotes forgiveness, easygoing treatment and healthy compromise to maintain love, peace and tranquillity. Overall, adopting a general attitude of gentleness in the family is far better than the habit of harshness and strictness, while still applying strictness where it is only needed and right. The Prophet ﷺ said, "Show gentleness, for if gentleness is found in anything, it beautifies it and when it is taken out from anything, it damages it."[84]

When it comes to our children, Allah ﷻ has commanded parents to treat them as a valuable trust which He placed in our care. They have rights over us, just as we have rights over them. The goal is to build and nurture our relationship with them through love and mercy. In addition to their rights of livelihood, day-to-day needs, protection and safety, they have the right to be taught the religion and the Qur'an both in recitation and in practice, receive beneficial education, to be named a good name, have their dignity respected, and have a good relationship with their parents and relatives. Successful parenting means to be aware and be accepting that as children grow older, their dependence on their parents

---

[84] Sunan Abi Dawud 4808, Book 43, *ḥadīth* 36

CONCLUSION

naturally becomes less and therefore parents should allow them to have more autonomy within reason and proportion. Parents should not resort to control in such a way that children feel deprived of their independence and personal privacy while developing through their teenage phase into adulthood.

It is important to consider that our children's generation differs from our own generation, and therefore we need to understand that certain cultural norms we grew up on may not suit our children. The key is to listen to their needs and exercise patience in attempting to see matters from their viewpoints and not just ours. Even though a parent may not agree to all of their children's requests, allowing them to express their views will make them feel that they are heard and acknowledged. This strengthens the trust and allows for more open communication between them. Love and trust cannot be built by increasing rules and restrictions, but by being invested and involved in our children's interests, hobbies, and feelings through heart-to-heart conversations and even sometimes showing some vulnerability by sharing our own feelings and personal stories. It is crucial to be aware that children will mirror their parents' behaviour and actions far more than listening and obeying their instructions and rules, so it is essential that they put role modelling at the forefront of raising children.

When it comes to parents' rights, the Quran and the prophetic tradition direct us to focus on our actions and treatment towards them. The command to be dutiful and kind to them is tremendous to the point of lowering our wing of humility and avoiding even pronouncing the expression 'ouff' to them. There is a difference between obeying everything they say and being dutiful, respectful and kind to them. Their right is that their children obey them in matters concerning their personal needs, and on anything else as long as it does not violate other people's rights or violates Allah's rights.

We need to be clear that in Islam, there is no right of obedience for any creation at the expense of disobedience to the Creator. For any other matter, a child must do what they can to the best of their abilities in obeying their parents. While some parents may be harsh or oppressive, it is still an obligation to maintain their rights if there is no danger or serious harm to the person. In those cases, a person may distance themselves to a safe degree but should still maintain their parents' rights within their capacity, even if it becomes limited due to these factors. The dutifulness to parents extends beyond their lifespan and after their death.

CONCLUSION

The Rights of Parents after Death are Five:

1. To supplicate for them.

2. To seek Allah's forgiveness for them.

3. To carry out their Islamically valid bequests.

4. To connect the family ties that are because of them.

5. To be kind to their friends who are still alive.

This is, of course, if it is within one's capacity and in the absence of perceived harm.

After marriage, in-laws become part of the circle of good treatment because of the spousal relationship. Although it is not legally legislated in Islam to serve in-laws, it is considered a high virtue and a praiseworthy feature of a Muslim husband or wife's character to offer good services towards them. This not only brings them closer to their in-laws, but also nurtures the love and closeness between spouses, leading to a healthy upbringing of their children. At times, conflict and tension may arise between in-laws, and the key is for spouses to agree together on strategies and approaches to deal with them. A good principle to follow is separating the roles, boundaries, rights and duties between what is for spouses, in-laws and other people.

Furthermore, if the relationship between in-laws becomes unhealthy or certain conflicts become unresolvable, the *Sharīʿah* has given allowance for each of the husband and wife to maintain a healthy distance. In these circumstances however, it is still advised in Islam to maintain any possible connection and communication with the in-laws, even if it is limited to religious and family occasions and special events. Children must never be involved in such situations and be allowed to keep their relationships with their grandparents, relatives and cousins. Reconciliation to whatever achievable extent, is always encouraged in the Quran.

The nucleus of the family is the husband and wife. They allow what comes into their lives and what stays outside of their lives, homes and relationships. Adopting the five Ts – trust, transparency, tolerance, time, and talking between each other is an excellent foundation to follow to nurture tranquillity and peace at home. Therefore, when they agree to live together on the principles of fearing Allah ﷻ in private and public, Allah ﷻ blesses them with *mawaddah* and *rahmah*, mutual understanding, sharing each other's lives in their property, time, sacrifices, physical and emotional dynamics, and respecting each other's dignity, rights and boundaries.

May Allah ﷻ bless every family, guide them to what is

CONCLUSION

pleasing to Him in this life and next, protect their children from all harm in their faith and identity, grant parents strength, patience and wisdom, make their marriages a goodness in this life and a pathway to Paradise in the Hereafter, and make us among those about whom Allah ﷻ said the following:

جَنَّـٰتُ عَدْنٍ يَدْخُلُونَهَا وَمَن صَلَحَ مِنْ ءَابَآئِهِمْ وَأَزْوَٰجِهِمْ وَذُرِّيَّـٰتِهِمْ وَٱلْمَلَـٰٓئِكَةُ يَدْخُلُونَ عَلَيْهِم مِّن كُلِّ بَابٍ ٢٣ سَلَـٰمٌ عَلَيْكُم بِمَا صَبَرْتُمْ فَنِعْمَ عُقْبَى ٱلدَّارِ ٢٤

'The Ever-lasting Gardens which they shall enter and so shall the righteous from among their fathers, and their spouses, and their offspring. And angels shall enter unto them from every gate and say: "Peace be upon you. You merit this reward for your steadfastness." How excellent is the ultimate abode![85]

---

85 Surah ar-Ra'd 13: 23-24